ALL MEN ARE DESPERATE... WHETHER THEY KNOW ~~KNOW~~ *ADMIT* IT OR NOT

WALTER SPIRES

All Men Are Desperate Whether They ~~Know~~ Admit It or Not Copyright © 2016 by Walter Spires. All rights reserved. This book or any portion thereof may not be reproduced or used in any manner whatsoever without the express written permission of the publisher except for the use of brief quotations embodied in reviews and certain other noncommercial uses permitted by copyright law.

Scripture quotations marked (NLT) are taken from the Holy Bible, New Living Translation, copyright © 1996, 2004, 2007 by Tyndale House Foundation. Used by permission of Tyndale House Publishers, Inc., Carol Stream, Illinois 60188. All rights reserved.

Scripture quotations taken from the New American Standard Bible (NASB), Copyright © 1960, 1962, 1963, 1968, 1971, 1972, 1973, 1975, 1977, 1995 by The Lockman Foundation. Used by permission. www.Lockman.org

Scripture quotations marked "KJV" are taken from the King James Version of the Bible.

First Printing, 2016

For permissions or ordering information, please contact:
Desperate Men Publishing
www.desperatemen.org
info@desperatemen.org

Print ISBN: 978-0-9977185-0-8
E-Book ISBN: 978-0-9977185-1-5

Cover design by Music Row Creative

Printed in the United States of America

TABLE OF CONTENTS

DEDICATION v

ACKNOWLEDGMENTS vii

PROLOGUE ix

PART ONE: The Journey Into Desperate Places
- Chapter One   Five Desperate Men 11
- Chapter Two   Uncommon Denominators 25
- Chapter Three   "All Men are Desperate" 35
- Chapter Four   Five Roads That Lead Men into Desperate Places 44
- Chapter Five   Toll Roads – The Only Way Out. 55

PART TWO: The Journey through the Cross
- Chapter Six   Two Trials, One Verdict 63
- Chapter Seven   Your Final Appeal 71
- Chapter Eight   The Desperation of God 76

PART THREE: The Journey Home
- Chapter Nine   Lord, Make Me a Butterfly 87
- Chapter Ten   What We Learn from Butterflies Can Change the World ... 97
- Chapter Eleven   Evidence of Desperate Living 104
- Chapter Twelve   Five Desperate Men (Reprised) 113

EPILOGUE 125

DEDICATION

This book and *menistry* are dedicated to all the *desperate* men who have graced my life and left their imprint on it more than I could have ever imagined. I began this ministry to give, teach, and serve men whose lives appeared more desperate and needy than mine. Not long into it, I found I received more than I gave, learned more than I taught, and was served in greater measure than that which I brought to the table.

Specifically, I want to thank the men in the life recovery programs of the Nashville Rescue Mission and Men of Valor prison ministry for helping me see my own desperate state as you seek deliverance from yours. Together we daily learn that only through utter dependence on God our Father, who loves unconditionally, Jesus our Savior, who saves completely, and the Holy Spirit, who comforts and guides us into all Truth, can we ever find the help, healing, and hope we so desperately seek. I am also grateful to the faithful staff and leadership of both for providing me these special opportunities to breathe into the lives of these men in a small way.

With my deepest gratitude and fondest affection, I write these words to the glory of God and dedicate them to you.

ACKNOWLEDGMENTS

I am, without a doubt, a most desperate man in my own right – desperately grateful that my gracious God and Father poured out His love and grace on me through my Savior and Lord Jesus Christ. I know that kind of statement can roll with relative ease from the tongues of those who feel like it is the right thing to say at such times. But I want to say from the bottom of my heart and depth of my soul, I mean every word of that.

Jesus said, "Apart from me you can do nothing." And, of course, He was right. I found, in and of my own doing, the best I could do was move from one desperate place to another. When Jesus took control of all that I would surrender to Him and poured out His Spirit on me, the real transformation in my life began and continues today – a work in progress.

I am also a man blessed with a great wife of more than three decades now. Gigi and I have enjoyed memorable times and endured a lot throughout the years from too many relocations to business failures that created considerable financial challenge. Satan has done his best to tear apart that which God joined together that blistering hot Memphis day in August of 1983.

There are not many things better than being a dad, especially after the start we had in that area. You will read part of our story and how God faithfully blessed us with three amazing kids, Trey, Gracie, and Zach. I am glad God chose me to be their dad. They are great encouragement to me. Steve and Sara have now joined our family through marriage. Gigi and I are "grands in waiting"!

With regard to the Desperate Men *menistry* and this book, there are a number of people, without whose prayer, financial support, and encouragement, neither would have gotten off the ground nor become sustainable. That list begins with my accountability partner of many years, Tom Eberle, and includes Kenny Hancock, John Hartong, Barry Webb, Todd Sorensen, Brett Cornelius, Erik Daniels, Gracie-Steve Moakler, Hank Coviello, Mike Law, David McClellan, Todd Kabel, Scott Farrar, John McClellan, Chris Taylor, Larry Kloess, Jeff Koch, and others who have since joined our team. I am also grateful to Marcus Martin, my friend and MOV staff member, who has been both an encouragement and inspiration to me.

Finally, and specifically regarding this book, *Desperate Men*, I am deeply grateful and indebted to Dave Boehi and his amazing God-given skills as an editor *par excellence*. I am truly amazed how God brought this gifted man, whom I met and served alongside for a short time more than twenty-six years ago, back into my life to help with this project. I am convinced the Lord's hand was on this re-connection after more than twenty-five years. He provided outstanding editorial advice and made this work better in every sense of the word.

"Now to Him who is able to do far more abundantly beyond all we ask or think, according to the power that works within us, to Him be the glory in the church and in Christ Jesus to all generations forever and ever." Amen.   Ephesians 3: 20-21 NASB

PROLOGUE

"What is a desperate man?", someone recently asked me. One might assume as the man who named this men's ministry, *Desperate Men*, I would have come up with a good definition. The truth is I have not. But I can show you what desperate men look like and that is far more important.

Being *desperate* means different things to different men, some good and others not so good. Consider these examples:

- Some men are desperate for success
- Some men are desperate for recognition
- Some are desperate to be included
- Some are desperate to find purpose or meaning in life
- Some are desperate to be loved
- Some are desperate to be a good husband or dad
- Some are desperate for more

For many men, our journeys into desperate places are smooth and downhill. We would be better off if such roads were harder to find and travel. Unfortunately, more often than not, that is not the case.

The journey *out* of desperation is polar opposite. As smooth and downhill as the road into desperate places may be, the road out is rough and uphill. Nor is it a straight road. There are many turns and, at each one, decisions have to be made. Our decisions, and the consequences that accompany them, ultimately determine our outcomes in life.

Desperate Men is a book that takes you on a journey through your life. This journey consists of three parts. Each part was developed to help us ask and answer some of life's hard questions. Questions about yourself. Questions about life. Questions about God.

We begin our journey with the stories of five men who come from completely different places and positions in life. But at some point in their journeys, they shared at least one thing in common: **each found himself at a desperate place in life facing difficult decisions.**

My friend, we are all *desperate men*. Lean in closely as you read and listen to what God is saying to you. If you are like most of us, you find yourself in one of three places in life:
- You may be desperate and without hope, stumbling through life without any relationship with God even though He loves you completely and unconditionally.
- Having taken your own roads, you may find yourself in a desperate place and need to find your way back to His outstretched arms.
- As a soldier of the Cross of Christ, you may be desperate for more of God. You may want to know what it looks like to live desperately all the way Home.

Regardless of who you are, where you are, or what you have done, I have good news. *Your life matters to God.* He simply calls you to come. *Come in. Come closer. Come up higher.*

Desperate Men was written to help you understand and answer that call. I pray these words find their way into your heart to bring the *help*, *healing*, and *hope* in Christ all men *desperately* need.

CHAPTER ONE
_____

Five Desperate Men

Warning: Statistics ahead! I understand the risk associated with beginning a book with a set of very sobering statistics. To hold your attention, read each one with this thought in mind:

<u>*Each number represents a man with a name.*</u>

You or me. Our sons, brothers, or dads. Neighbors. Co-workers. Each of us knows at least one man who is or was on such a list. Personalizing these numbers causes us to read them with more compassion. It also instills the fear of God that one of us or our sons might be found among them.

- SUICIDE: According to the Centers for Disease Control and Prevention, about *eighty* men will commit suicide today. A strong possibility exists a desperate man took his life as you read this. Families, the real victims, are left with unanswered questions and grief unspeakable. Sadly these men die without hope, believing no one cares. But God does.

- ADDICTION: Eleven million men battle alcohol, drug, pornography, and other addictions. Most men struggle with these demons in secret. Some of you are in that battle now.

- PRISON: More than 2 million men are incarcerated, the highest number and percent in the world—40 - 70 percent are from fatherless homes. The recidivism rate is 67 - 80 percent; meaning they return to prison after they are released. Many of their sons will follow.
- DIVORCE: Over 1.2 million men got divorced last year. We are told around 40 percent of those were "Christian marriages." Some of you have "been there, done that."
- HOMELESS: More than 400,000 homeless men live in America. Many gave up and lost hope. These "faceless" people include former neighbors, classmates, family with whom you lost touch. If the market tanks (again), some of you may join them.

Whether you or someone close to you is counted among those statistics, I have good news for you. Here are three encouraging storylines you will not find in mainstream media:

> ✟ *God loves us no matter what we did, where we are, why we left, or how we got there.*
> ✟ *God's 24/7/365 helpline is only a prayer away. No busy signals or voice mail here.*
> ✟ *Hope abounds for all who are in Christ. All are welcome. Meet at the foot of the cross.*

With those thoughts in mind, let's begin our journey. We do so by looking in on five men from very different walks of life—each of whom will face difficult decisions, more similar to the ones we confront than we care to admit.

The Addict
Many addicts are nameless and faceless to us. To most of us who live miles away in better zip codes, they are invisible.

James was one of those invisible men. But he did not start out that way. No child begins life with the thought or ambition of one day finding himself a victim of and slave to one of many addictions that plague men today. I chose both of these words intentionally because addicts are often victims who become slaves. That was the case with our friend, James.

James started out life in a hard place that only got harder. That hardly seems possible when you are born on a concrete floor like James. He was what we would call a "high-risk child"—born into a low-income world of poverty to a mother who did not welcome him. She had crack issues and was not certain who James' dad was, nor did she seem to care.

Babies like James have a much higher probability of experiencing abuse and getting into trouble early in life—drugs and alcohol, violence, dropping out of school, and incarceration. Staying alive becomes a challenge for many, so they turn to gang life.

Despite the horrible environment in which he began life, James was very likeable and considered a good kid by most people in the 'hood. He was helpful and eager to please. The latter would contribute to his undoing as he moved into his teen years. James also developed great survival instincts that served him well. That is, after all, what his life was all about ... survival.

Like many of us during our teen years, James' desire to please and be included led him to make the decision to follow the crowd. Unfortunately for him, it was the wrong crowd. Peer pressure is such a strong force in our lives during that season. The fact that "everyone" was doing it led James to become a recreational drug and alcohol user. Continued use finally caused him to drop school just ahead of being suspended for the last time.

On the street with nowhere to turn, it was as if James stepped in quicksand. He knew he was sinking but could not climb out by himself and had no one to help. His recreational drug and alcohol use slowly increased and eventually turned into dependency. Like his mother, James was now an addict.

To feed his need, James began to deal drugs. Scared, tired, and alone, James finally looked himself in the mirror and, for the first time in his life, saw himself for what he had become – a truly *desperate man*.

The Prisoner

Joe Jr. entered this world nineteen years ago on a very cold winter night in an inner city hospital. His birth came at the expense of a long, hard labor for his mother. This symbolized his life to follow.

His dad, Joe Sr., could not be there for the birth of his son. He was serving five - ten for dealing drugs (again). Before prison, he had a job in the local factory working on the line for not much more than minimum wage. Men with records have a hard time getting any job. Dealing drugs paid better than his day job, but it is high risk/reward work and landed him back in prison.

Joe Jr.'s mother wanted the best for her son. As he grew up, she did her best to keep him away from gang culture. However, like many single moms or wives of incarcerated men, she worked two jobs to pay bills and support her children. That kept her away from home, leaving Joe Jr. unsupervised with too much time on his hands. The bad guys in the 'hood were only too happy to help fill that time.

Pressure to join gangs can be overpowering for teenaged boys in Joe Jr.'s circumstances. He had a decision to make. He made a bad one and the rest, as they say, is history. This was the beginning of his story, the one his mother had worked so hard to prevent.

Young men whose fathers are in prison are five times more likely to go themselves. In Joe Jr.'s case, this statistic held true. Caught up in gang violence and convicted for his part, at the ripe young at of nineteen, Joe Jr. entered prison for the first time.

Once inside, JJ, as the other inmates referred to him, found life a lot like that on the outside except he had a regular place to eat and sleep. JJ met with many of the same temptations and social issues that cost him his freedom. And irony of ironies, JJ was now doing time in the same prison as his father. This is where JJ's life took a decided turn.

During his latest incarceration, Joe Sr. came to a desperate place. His hard life finally brought him to the end of himself. He was a man full of deep regret and remorse at the mess he made of his life and the legacy he was leaving his children.

This is where God stepped into Joe Sr.'s life. He knew for years there was an onsite prison ministry. But like many of the other prisoners, he often made fun of the men in it who "found Jesus and made Him warden of their lives." But now, desperate for help, he attended a meeting, and there for the first time he heard words of love, life, and freedom. He left with something he never felt before, a strange sense of peace and hope.

God loves bringing men to desperate places. After several meetings, he surrendered his hard-fought life to Christ and began to understand and experience freedom for the first time in his life, even though he remained behind bars.

When Joe Sr. learned his son had joined him in prison, he grieved with a sorrow so deep nearly every man in his cellblock could hear him weeping and crying out to God. He was determined to make things right with JJ. He wanted to build a relationship that had never existed, and most of all introduce him to Jesus. Easier said than done.

Years of watching his mother work so hard to provide and knowing his dad always seemed to in jail, JJ had become a bitter, angry young man.

He wanted nothing to do with his father. His father was as good as dead to him. Joe Sr. tried his best to get time with his son, but JJ would have none of that. He was consumed with anger, bitterness, and resentment, thrashing his way through life. So Joe Sr. did the best thing any desperate dad can do for his son, given the circumstances. He got on his knees every day in his cell and prayed for his son.

The Rich Man
Rich men come by their wealth in a number of interesting ways. Some are born into wealthy families; their wealth comes as a birthright. Others gain wealth because they are in the right place at the right time. For example, they may work for a company that grows tremendously and delivers wealth through stock appreciation. Then there are men whose hard work ("sweat equity") pays off, and they amass great wealth. Regardless of how men acquire their wealth, it is very easy to fall into the trap of allowing bank balances to define them as men.

Charles was born January 7, 1978 and instantly became a multimillionaire. It was as if he won the lottery and did not even have to purchase a ticket. Charles' parents were not only wealthy, but also highly influential in the community, socially involved, and connected.

Charles went to the right schools, wore the right clothes, and generally did everything well a rich kid was supposed to do. Growing up, his family was not close. His father worked long hours, while his mother stayed busy donating time and money to community services. Church was an afterthought and matter of convenience.

An only child, Charles had great expectations placed upon him and the accompanying pressure he neither welcomed nor tolerated very well. Soon after prep school graduation, Charles did what many tightly reined kids do when they leave the nest and begin to experience freedom for the first time—he partied his way through an expensive undergraduate education. On one occasion, he had to invoke his father's considerable influence to secure ongoing enrollment. (I suspect a large donation was made to the school!)

Upon graduation, Charles once again did what was expected by joining the family business. It was not what he wanted, but it was the best way to remain in the good graces of his father and continue a lifestyle he had come to enjoy. Charles started at the bottom of the company ladder along with the other fresh grads. Despite the "silver spoon," Charles was a conscientious, hard worker who quickly rose in the ranks to no one's surprise.

Like most sons, Charles secretly yearned for his father's approval. A hug, pat on the back, word of encouragement or expression of pride in him or his work would have fed Charles' great need for acceptance. Unfortunately, his father was an aloof man not given to the demonstrations of emotion or expressions of love. He justified his *workaholism* as the means to keep the family fortunes and way of life intact. His god was his wealth, and he served it well.

Despite his hard work, wealth, and position, Charles' father's story did not end well. When the market crashed in 2008 and most of the family fortune was lost, he fell into a deep depression. His social use of alcohol turned habitual. The downhill slide became an avalanche he could no longer manage or tolerate. For the first time in his life, Charles' father was a desperate man. Unable to cope and too proud to ask for help, one cold January night he took his own life.

The aftermath of such profoundly sad decisions carry devastating consequences. In this case, *one desperate man died leaving another behind.*

Despite the fact that they were not a close family, Charles and his mother were highly distraught at the loss. Charles took the death of his father particularly hard. He never received his father's blessing, so the approval he desperately sought was now forever withheld.

Charles was left to sort through the aftermath of his father's suicide and consider how all of this would affect him as a man, husband, and father of his own children. He was desperate for answers but had nowhere to turn.

Charles turned to the same gods his father served so well … work and wealth. He took great pride in both. Charles worked night and day to rebuild the family business and restore their financial fortunes. Nothing was going to stand in his way. Charles had his father's knack for making money and enjoyed great success. Like father, like son? Only time will tell.

The Pastor
Thomas was blessed in a way kids do not appreciate until they are adults with their own children. He was raised in a Christian home, regularly attended church and youth group, and was generally considered a great kid. Because of these strong influences, Thomas decided in high school to become a pastor. He told everyone he felt the "calling of the Lord" on his life. His parents and church family were very excited. Friends were a bit skeptical.

Thomas had somewhat of a storybook life. In college, he married his high school sweetheart. After graduation she worked to help put him through seminary. Upon completion of his divinity degree, Thomas accepted a position with a well-known mega-church. His ministry career was off to a great start. Another blessing came later that year as their first child lit up their lives.

Thomas studied and prepared well in seminary. He was well-grounded in doctrine and biblical theology and also very articulate. That combination led to his rise within the pastoral staff and favor with the church. Within a few years, Thomas was asked to become the senior pastor of a small, growing church. The church was located in a great part of the city with a lot of young families like his. He and his wife enthusiastically accepted.

If this story seems almost too good to be true, it is. During his seminary years, Thomas spent many hours on the Internet buried in its files and scouring websites. One night while preparing a paper, Thomas inadvertently typed in an incorrect URL and found himself on a pornographic website.

Having grown up somewhat sheltered and naïve, his eyes could not believe what they were seeing. He knew he should immediately close the site and move on. But there was something intoxicating about the graphic images that held his attention far too long. Sadly, this simple typographical error could one day destroy his family and ministry.

Desperate to keep his secret sin secret, Thomas did everything he could to hide his shame, but did not feel enough remorse or conviction to ask for help. Pastors who teach through the Bible as Thomas did often find themselves speaking about sins like lusts of the flesh. But even as he encouraged his congregation to turn aside from these temptations, he continued to rationalize and hide his actions.

During the next few years, the church continued to experience rapid growth. Thomas was also growing in popularity as a national speaker. He thought he had everything under control, restricting his pornographic viewing to the computer at home. The church network was protected by software designed to prevent staff from viewing inappropriate sites.

Then the unthinkable happened. When her iPad didn't work, Thomas' wife went into his study to use his computer to check Facebook. Much to her shock and dismay, she found herself looking at a porn site that Thomas forgot to close. She checked the URL history for previously visited sites and began to weep bitterly. After gathering herself, she went in to confront Thomas.

This was one of those moments in life no man wants to face, especially a Christian pastor. Confronted with his sin, Thomas knew he had jeopardized his marriage, family, church, and ministry. For the first time in his almost storybook life, Thomas found himself a truly desperate man in a very desperate place.

The Businessman

Men who travel extensively for business know it is anything but the glamorous life perceived by those left behind in the office. To the weary frequent traveler, the number of stars beside a hotel listing soon melt together in one pot – another flight to catch, another hotel room in another city, another night away from the family.

David was a successful sales manager for a high-growth tech company headquartered in Silicon Valley. He had a large territory that required a lot of airline travel and too many overnights. Much to his chagrin, and that of his wife, David was A-list, platinum, and other symbols of people who travel more than they would like and, perhaps for some, more than they should. But David made good money that supported a very comfortable lifestyle for his family. That seemed justification enough.

David married his college sweetheart. Smart and attractive, she represented her sorority in various talent and beauty pageants. They married the summer after both graduated from college. When their first child was born, they agreed she would set aside her short-lived career to focus full-time attention on their kids. David did well enough financially to keep up their lifestyle. Yes sir, David was a "blessed man," as he liked to refer to his life, marriage, and family.

As more kids came along, David found himself torn between the need to keep up financially and the fact that he really wanted to be home more. He chose the former, which turned out to be a very bad decision.

David's wife felt the increased strain of his frequent absence. She told friends she knew what it felt like to be a single parent. The pressure began to create friction between them. She became more vocal about her displeasure with his extensive travel schedule and noted he was not much help even when he was at home. His response was always the same. He had to travel like that to maintain their lifestyle, and he was tired when he got home.

Life on the road can take a heavy toll on men no matter how dedicated and faithful they are or how strongly they desire to remain so. Problems on the home front fan the sparks. Men begin to look for outlets or escapes from reality, so we let down our guards. When that happens, we become vulnerable to temptation.

"Road temptations" come in various forms and places. TV and Internet porn. Business meetings and dinners that facilitate close interactions with co-workers of the opposite sex. One night after a long day of meetings and too many drinks over dinner, David joined that inauspicious group we are told represents 22 percent of all married men. He was unfaithful to his wife.

The next day on the flight home, he was completely distraught. How would he look his tired and beleaguered wife in the eye? What would he say to her? Would he try to forget that it happened, put on a face of deceit, and begin the lies? Or would he come clean and begin a long overdue process of building, or rebuilding, his marriage?

Five different men. Five different journeys. The same destination. Each found himself in a desperate place in life—a place of helplessness; one from which they could not escape on their own. They were going to need help. The question is would they ever admit that and seek it.

Our tendency as men is to casually read such stories and blow them off as not particularly relevant to you and me. "I'm not a prisoner or an addict. I am not a pastor or rich. I have not had an affair."

We tend to focus on the *differences* between the men in the stories and ourselves, especially those traits or characteristics we do not like. I suggest we need to focus on those areas we may have in common. And that, my friend, is exactly what we are going to do in the next chapter.

Questions Every Desperate Man Needs to Answer

1) What is a desperate man? Please write your definition in the space below.
   _____
   _____
   _____

2) Why is the journey into desperate places so much easier than the roads out? Answer this from the point of view of the five men in the stories and your own journey.
   _____
   _____
   _____

From the stories of the five men, we learned:
- James struggles with addiction.
- Joe Jr. is a prisoner.
- Charles worships his wealth.
- Pastor Thomas hides secret sins.
- David is unfaithful to his wife and children.

3) What bad decision(s) did each man make that led him into a desperate place?
   James: _____
   _____
   _____

   Joe Jr: _____
   _____
   _____

   Charles: _____

Thomas:

David:

Personal Reflections on My Journey:

CHAPTER TWO

Uncommon Denominators

While each man is unique, we all share qualities, attributes, and issues *common* to other men. For example, we are sons who had fathers and mothers. Many of us are husbands and fathers. We may be alumni of the same schools, have kids that play on the same sports teams, or work for the same company. We typically refer to such things as "common denominators"– similarities that exist between men regardless of position in life, zip code, or bank balance.

I suggest another category exists that is more difficult to perceive between ourselves and other men. I refer to these as *uncommon denominators*—attributes or conditions we observe in the lives of other men with which we would take strong issue if someone suggested they exist in our lives. That is because they often carry negative implications or connotations.

To illustrate how this concept plays out, let's revisit our five friends from the previous chapter. Their brief biographical sketches led to the following conclusions:
- James struggles with addiction.
- Joe Jr. is a prisoner.
- Charles worships his wealth.

- Pastor Thomas hides secret sins.
- David is unfaithful to his wife and children.

All are desperate men. And though you may not realize or want to admit it, you may have something in common with one or more of them – *uncommon denominators*.

Addiction

We typically associate addiction with men who have significant substance abuse issues. Clearly that is a huge problem among men in our nation. Yet addiction goes further and deeper than substance abuse. Addiction is *the inability to exercise control or power over certain things or areas of our lives*. We do not control them. They control us.

It may surprise you to read that the Apostle Paul expressed concerns about problems with sinful areas of his own life. In Romans, he wrote,

> *"We know the law is spiritual; but I am unspiritual, sold as a slave to sin. I do not understand what I do. For what I want to do I do not do, but what I hate I do."*   Romans 7:14-15 NIV

I don't know about you, but I take some comfort from Paul's honest personal revelation and confession. I certainly find myself there at times and feel certain you do as well. The Apostle Peter expressed a similar thought in this way:

> *"...for by what a man is overcome, by this he is enslaved"*   2 Peter 2:19b NASB

Addiction is internal warfare. Some may argue Paul was not talking about addictions as we consider them today. However, he said clearly *he did what he did not want to do.* **We all have areas in our lives that control or seek to control us.**

Our friend, James, had obvious issues with addiction. Not all addictions are related to drugs, alcohol, or pornography. If we are honest, we will admit to more subtle addictions, less obvious to others, that seek to control us. In such areas, addiction becomes the *uncommon denominator*.

Prison

I have been blessed to have the privilege of teaching men in a cellblock who are part of a ministry dedicated to helping prisoners develop a relationship with Christ and grow in their faith. These men are incarcerated for any number of crimes to which most of us could not relate. However, I suggest all of us can relate to being prisoners of one form or another. Remember this line after you lay aside this book.
"Not all prisons have bars."

Some of us are imprisoned in executive offices or bad marriages. Others are prisoners of our pasts. The truth is desperate men are found on both sides of the prison bars. That makes prison an *uncommon denominator*.

Most inmates want out of prison. Men in *prisons without bars* also want out. Out of bad marriages. Out of bad or high stress jobs. Freedom or escape from their pasts. Some men grin and bear it. Others walk away. And a few make that devastating decision that should be God's alone. They decide to leave this world on their terms and by their own hands. They fail to consider that this kind of freedom leaves families in chains, imprisoned by thoughts and regrets, with many questions that remain forever unanswered.

For those of us on the "outside," we can walk out of our prisons any time we are ready. The question is, are you ready? If not, what are you doing to get ready? Jesus said He came to "set the prisoners free." Many men remain in prison who could be set free. Are you one of them?

Riches

Across our affluent nation, we find very wealthy people who live in gated communities surrounded by walls for protection and separation. Many men, who lack such financial affluence, envy those who do. And you might be surprised to learn there are rich people in those communities who are miserable despite their wealth…some because of it.

Jesus had a lot to say to rich people and about money in general. Many are familiar with the story of the rich young ruler in Matthew 19. This rich man asked Jesus what he had to do to get eternal life. After an exchange in which the man defended the good life he led, Jesus told him the only thing left was for him to sell all he owned, give it to the poor, and follow Jesus. The man was devastated; this was not the answer he expected.

> *"When the young man heard this he went away sad, because he had great wealth."* Matthew 19:22 NIV

After the rich man walked away, Jesus made the following statement that stunned all who heard it, including His disciples:

> *"Again I tell you, it is easier for a camel to go through the eye of a needle than for someone who is rich to enter the kingdom of God."* Matthew 19:24, NIV

Jesus' teachings on wealth give many rich men heartburn. They spend their lives building wealth, and the thought of liquidating their assets to give to the poor seems patently absurd.

Jesus told another story about wealth I consider His most profound teaching on the subject – the story of the rich fool.

> *"The land of a rich man was very productive. And he began reasoning to himself, saying, 'What shall I do, since I have no place to store my crops?' Then he said, 'This is what I will do: I will tear down my barns and build larger ones, and there I will store all my grain and my goods. And I will say to my soul, "Soul, you have many goods laid up for many years to come; take your ease, eat, drink and be merry."*
>
> Luke 12: 16-19 NASB

If we put this story into the context of today, sadly, we see when some men become wealthy they decide to build bigger houses, buy more of them, or acquire more "toys." Naturally, more stuff requires more storage.

The story did not end well for the rich man (fool) in the parable. God directly called him out for this foolish use of his increased wealth:

> *"You fool, this night your very life will be required of you, and now who will own what you have prepared?"* Luke 12:20 NASB

That is some of the strongest language you will find in the Bible, and it came straight from the mouth of God. Jesus ended this parable with very troubling words.

> *"This is how it will be with whoever stores up things for themselves but is not rich toward God."* Luke 12:20 NIV

While these are challenging passages for men of wealth, Jesus was not speaking only to men with large bank accounts. Most of us could be considered "rich" compared with much of the world today. Most of us have gathered many possessions (toys) over the years, and we enjoy their use whenever our busy lives afford us the time. We take pride in them. They represent the fruit of our labors. Let me make this point very clear.

> *The issue is not men who own possessions. Rather, it is men whose possessions own them.*

Rich, middle income, or poor by the world's standards, if that statement describes you, we have identified another *uncommon denominator*.

Let's end this with a direct question, similar to that which Jesus asked the rich young ruler.

> *"Do you own your possessions or do they own you?"*

The honest answer is found in our checkbooks (or Quicken file).

Secret Sins

One might consider it difficult to find common denominators between a pastor and men who are not "called" to the ministry. Let me assure you that pastors and ministers are ordinary people. They experience the same yearnings of the flesh, and the same temptation toward selfishness. And like all men, sometimes they fall. Because of their visibility and expectations from church members and the community at large, those falls can be very great and the landings very hard.

Pornography ranks among the highest and most frequent of *secret sins*. Like a stealth bomber, it glides in low and undetected until it is too late. We saw this with Pastor Thomas where it snuck in through a misspelled URL. Pornography plays on one of the great pleasures God created and intended for men, sexual pleasure. The apostle John listed *"the lust of the flesh and the lust of the eyes"* as two of three primary categories of sins in the world today. Both contribute to pornography addiction. The third type, *"pride of life,"* keeps men enslaved, too proud and ashamed to confess it.

Yet pornography is only one of the secret sins men harbor. Secret sins are areas of our lives we deliberately hide from others and *think* we hide from God. They include *thoughts* and *behaviors* that, if exposed, could create issues, some serious, for the man hiding them. You and I are not immune. In fact, chances are a number of you harbors some type of secret sin in your life.

Secret sins in our own lives, regardless of their origin and whether or not they have been revealed, represent our *uncommon denominator* with Pastor Thomas.

Adultery
Adultery is almost always thought of as sexual sin in marriage. While that is the most prolific use of the term, it is not the only one. Apart from the obvious definition, adultery also means *unfaithfulness* and *infidelity (disloyalty)*. On many occasions throughout the Old Testament, God accused the nation of Israel of "playing the harlot" because they had "adulterous" relationships with pagan nations and their false gods. They were unfaithful to God—they set Him aside and worshiped other deities. Here is one example.

> *"As for your adulteries and your lustful neighings, the lewdness of your prostitution on the hills in the field, I have seen your abominations. Woe to you, O Jerusalem! How long will you remain unclean?"*
> Jeremiah 13:27 NASB

God considered the ongoing unfaithfulness of the nation of Israel an "abomination." That is the strongest of language. Ultimately Israel's unrelenting and unrepentant behavior led to her destruction and captivity. The nation of Israel was no more for thousands of years. Jesus blew it up even further when He said,

> *"But I tell you that anyone who looks at a woman lustfully has already committed adultery with her in his heart."* Matthew 5:28 NIV

That is a serious charge and probably covers every man reading this. You thought because your lustfulness was only "wishful thinking," you were clear on that front. Bad news. Jesus indicted all of us whose minds have wandered in that way.

So we all have an *uncommon denominator* with our much-traveled businessman friend, David. We all have been guilty of adultery, whether we admit it or not.

Questions Every Desperate Man Needs to Answer

1) *"Addiction is the inability to exercise control or power over certain things or areas of our lives. We do not control them. They control us."* James had a drug addiction. What are some of the less obvious kinds of addictions that capture, control, or overcome men?

2) *"Not all prisons have bars."* Are there areas in your life in which you are in a *prison without bars*? What are you doing to get free or break those chains?

3) *"The issue is not rich men who own possessions. It is men, regardless of the size of their bank account, whose possessions own them."* Do you own your possessions or do they own you? What did Jesus say makes a man rich?

4) *"Secret sins are areas of our lives we deliberately hide from others and think we hide from God."* What are other "secret sins" men hide besides pornography? Are there any in your life that need to be exposed and dealt with?

5) *"Adultery is not just marital infidelity."* What other kinds of adultery do men commit? Are there any such "affairs" in your life that you need to confess before God to restore your relationship with Him?

Personal Reflections on My Journey:

CHAPTER THREE

"All Men Are Desperate Whether They ~~Know~~ Admit It or Not"

I think it is safe to say every man has his own *desperate man* story. Most of us have more than one. For me, one sticks out more than any other. This book would not be complete if I did not share it with you. It has nothing to do with what many would consider more typical desperate stories—no adultery, drugs, alcohol, porn, etc. But I was at a desperate place nonetheless.

It was October 4, 1985, a very pleasant fall day in Germantown, Tenn. I was laying two on a long par five on the East Course of Wyndyke Country Club. I was actually in the fairway for a change and thinking birdie on a hole I normally would have been delighted to par. I had taken the day off work to play a round with a friend to help calm my nerves and distract my mind from the imminent delivery of our first child. I awaited a call from my wife, Gigi, to let me know it was time to go to the hospital.

Before I teed off, I asked my good friend the head pro to sound the weather warning air horn in the event my wife called him. Her parents were also on call. (We did not have cell phones in those days.) Since we had seen her obstetrician a day or so before, we were comfortable this was a good plan. So with her encouragement, I headed to the course.

Memphis summers are known for being long, hot, and humid. That one was no exception. The heat and humidity can be oppressive at times and make that last trimester of pregnancy even more challenging. My wife was more than ready for this delivery as are all woman who endure those nine long months from conception to birth. She was particularly ready for this delivery.

For many young married couples, infertility can be a real issue. That was not our problem. We had no problem with my wife getting pregnant. *Staying* pregnant was the issue…a huge one. During a span of a little over a year, Gigi suffered a first-semester miscarriage three times. I confess looking back on those difficult days it was much harder on my wife, both physically and emotionally.

One physician told us we would not be able to have kids because she simply could not stay pregnant. We sought another opinion of an expert in the area and he assured us that was not the case. So in January 1985 my wife became pregnant a fourth time, and this time by the grace of God and a lot of staying horizontal, she carried the baby to full term. We were obviously ecstatic with joy and anticipation.

In her last pre-birth exam, we asked the doctor to go ahead and induce labor because she was close to her due date. He assured us there was no need to do that and the baby would come on its own any day.

I think I pulled out an 8-iron, preparing to hit my third shot, when my head pro friend drove up in a golf cart. All he said was, "Get in. Your wife is on the way to the hospital." I was stunned to say the least. I do not remember the ride back to my car. I do remember the drive to the hospital.

Driving as fast as I could, I pulled into the hospital emergency room parking lot. I ran in, found her room, and immediately knew something was very wrong. Gigi was lying in bed and, sobbing through her tears, told me, "The baby's dead. I'm so sorry. The baby's dead." I remember holding her a while, both of us in shock. I really don't remember if I cried then, but I cried a lot later.

The worst part, especially for Gigi, was going through labor to deliver a baby whose crying would not bring her into this world and whose smile we would not see this side of Heaven. Our little girl was already home with the Lord. So there I sat in the hospital room alongside my young wife who was absolutely crushed and now asked to go through this incredible ordeal. Four pregnancies in two years and not one live birth.

Tears still fall freely every time I tell or write this story. You never fully recover from events like that. Even as a young couple, we both had a strong faith in God, and we really never questioned Him on things, trusting in His sovereignty. But times like those make desperate people of us all. I am no exception. I remember later that night sitting in a chair holding my lifeless daughter, sobbing. There was nothing I could do as a man to fix this problem. I could only cry out to God, numb and desperate.

As in my own story, we left each of our five friends – the addict, prisoner, rich man, pastor, and businessman – at a desperate place in his life. Each of these men faces difficult decisions going forward and the potential consequences that accompany previous ones that brought them here.

Neither I nor any of these five men expected to end up in such a desperate place. The decisions we make and how we deal with the difficult circumstances will determine, in large part, future successes or failures.

Two Groups of Desperate Men

For many years, I have been blessed to teach and hang out with men most people consider desperate men in desperate places. They reside in rescue missions, life recovery programs for substance abuse and addiction, prison, and aftercare programs.

I also teach and hang out with men from the suburbs through business and church. Their outward appearance is anything but desperate. But all men know outward appearance can be a front or façade for desperate hearts within.

At some point in the life of every man, regardless of position or place, we look up one day and find ourselves in a *desperate* place—a circumstance, or destination we did not expect. A situation we are unable to fix no matter how hard we try. Men who contend they are not or have not been desperate are either very blessed or deceiving themselves. The question is not whether or not we are all desperate men. The question is whether or not we will admit it!

Decades of working with men from all walks of life led me to conclude we fall into two groups.

1) Men who are desperate and admit it.
2) Men who are desperate and will not admit it.

Group One: Men Who Are Desperate and Admit It

Men who fall into this category are a blessing and joy to be around. I am not saying they woke up one day with the revelation they were desperate men. More often than not, that realization comes from lessons learned through a difficult situation or personal failure. We could say they "graduated" to a better place, one in which facades are torn down and denial confronted. Contrition and humility become more visible as arrogance and pride fade to gray.

Consider the men most often thought to be desperate—those with substance or related issues who show up at rescue missions or get sent to prison. Some of these men arrive broken, needy, and completely aware of their desperate state. They have bottomed out and know it. Not much stands between them and an early, ugly death or a life no man wants to lead. Feeling hopeless and wanting to stop the downward spiral, they look for help.

When they arrive at the doors of one of these life recovery programs, they meet men who also came in broken, but by God's grace and others investing in their lives, they found help and healing. Because of their own battles with similar issues, these victorious men are able to demonstrate the love and concern these addicts and prisoners have never known. Perhaps most importantly, they try to help restore the hopes of these desperate men.

On the other side of town, the word *desperate* is seldom associated with men of means. By the world's standard, they are anything but desperate because they possess so much more in terms of financial and material blessing than most. They seem to have it made.

One of the things I find both encouraging and exciting is when I meet with men of substantial means who possess humble and thankful hearts. They became generous givers because they understand God provided their abundance; it is not something they deserved. They are great examples of obedience to Jesus' command,

> *"From everyone who has been given much, much will be demanded"*
> Luke 12:48 NIV

These men live graciously with an understanding that God owns all they possess and has made them *stewards* for a season to use His resources as He would. They are also desperate men. Not desperate for more, because they have so much. They are desperate to live a life that pleases God as they use their abundance to bless others.

Group Two: Men Who Are Desperate and Will Not Admit It

There is another group of men who show up at rescue missions or enter prisons with 'tudes, bad ones. They are angry, resentful, and often defensive. They believe the world has not treated them fairly. Life owes them something, so they take it when they can.

Failure to admit their desperate state and get the help they need to deal with addictions and related issues keeps another subset of these men homeless or hanging around outside rescue missions waiting for a free meal. It is a sad situation as these men are very hard to reach. To most observers, they are desperate men in every sense of the word. Yet they refuse to admit it, or perhaps they are blind to the truth.

There are also many other men just as desperate in their own way. The difference is they do not look desperate on the outside—men who hold good jobs, are committed to their families, and serve as leaders in their churches and communities. Highly successful men. Or are they?

These men would object strongly to my assertion that they are desperate and to any inclusion among or comparison to men found in rescue missions or prisons. They might agree those are d*esperate*, but they certainly do not identify with them in any way.

I do not just suggest the following; I say with certainty that these men have not yet come to the end of themselves. Until they do, they will not admit they are also desperate men.

The following story reveals in part the faithfulness of God to lead Gigi and me out of that desperate place I left us earlier in the chapter. The Lord did indeed bless us with three amazing children, and this comical anecdote is from one of my best memories of my youngest son.

I laugh out loud when I remember some of the antics of my youngest son when he was a little boy. The youngest of three, he came up with strategies to avoid getting in trouble when caught in the act. For example, when confronted with his misdeeds or one of his trails of destruction (or cookie crumbs), he went into his act. "Sorry, daddy. Sorry. Sorry."

He hoped the apologies would be viewed as repentance for his behavior. He also hoped he could avoid the discipline we used in those years, including spanking. Unfortunately for him, it did not work. *My son was not sorry. He was just sorry he got caught!*

The same may be said of men in this second group who show up at rescue missions or in prison. When caught in the act of some misdeed or unlawful act, they are not sorry. They are just sorry (or angry, resentful, etc.) they got caught. They often come up with excuses or blame others.

On the other side of town, the same may be said about some men of means. When things do not go their way or they are caught in unethical or illegal business dealings, they also blame others or call their attorneys, something their poor counterparts cannot afford.

Likewise, if secret sins like adultery or pornography are exposed or they are repeatedly found under the influence of alcohol or drugs, they rationalize their failings without accepting any responsibility or owning their actions. Again, not sorry. Just sorry they were caught.

God knows the difference between men who flippantly express sorrow and those who demonstrate what the Bible calls "*godly sorrow that brings repentance*" (2 Corinthians 7:10). God does not force men to see things His way or follow His plan for their lives. He allows us to rebel and go our own way. But those who choose foolishly eventually end up on roads that lead to desperate places.

As in a bad dream, men who choose their own roads often wake up to find themselves in places they never intended to visit. They had good intentions of exiting before the road became rough and took them into dark and desperate places.

We have all been in desperate places at some point in our lives, wondering how we got there, what holds us there, and how we can find a way out. The next chapter addresses *roads* that lead us into desperate places, how we can identify them in our own lives, and some of the consequences of each.

Questions Every Desperate Man Needs to Answer

1) *"Men who are desperate and admit it."* What are the two key characteristics or attributes that become evident in this group of men? Give examples of things or events in a man's life that bring him to this place. Have there been any such defining moments in your life you can share?

   1._____ and   2._____

   _____
   _____

2) *"Men who are desperate and will not admit it."* What are some of the issues that put (and keep) men in this group? What does it take for a man to move from Group 2 into Group 1? In which group do you consider yourself? Are there still things that hold you in Group 2?

   _____
   _____

Personal Reflections on My Journey:

_____
_____
_____

CHAPTER FOUR

Five Roads That Lead Men into Desperate Places

You have not been married very long or driven somewhere new on a family vacation if you have not heard the following from your wife: "We're lost. Why don't you stop and ask directions?"

I remember a family trip to Disney World years ago. I had no trouble finding my way in, but somewhere on the way out I obviously made a wrong turn. I learned the hard way that Disney World is a massive piece of property! My kids got to see areas of the park most people never venture into—the backside, outside the fences and walls! I found myself thinking, "How did I end up here?"

Most of the time when we get in the car and hit the road we have already decided where we are going. Work. Church. Ball game. Vacation. Kids' activities. We also know which roads will take us there. Unfortunately, that is not always the case in life. Sometimes we think we know where we are going but bad decisions lead us to surprising, even desperate places.

We began this journey looking into the lives of five men who represent a good cross-section of men in our country. Bad decisions left each one in a desperate place and at a crossroad in his life.

To help us examine the things that affect and influence our decisions, I want to spend some time drilling down on what led each of our five friends to make the bad decisions that left them in desperate faces, staring down the consequences. Then we will consider five other men with similar root causes to their problems, men whose stories are found in the pages of the Bible. Finally, we will put ourselves under the glass to do a little introspection.

Fear. James ended up an addict like his mother, but recall he began life as a likeable kid who just wanted to please people and find acceptance. Fear entered his life at an early age. Fear his mother would abandon him as his father had. Fear he would end up like her. Fear that other kids would not like or accept him into their groups.

The positive side of fear is it makes us more aware of dangers and cognizant of our surroundings. But the downside seems to dominate. Fear leads men into desperate places perhaps more than any other. Fear of failure tops the list for most of us. Others include fear of the unknown and fear of what others think. There are so many examples in the Bible of men who demonstrated *fear* on a number of fronts, their stories could fill another book.

To discuss the *fear* factor, I chose to focus on one setting, a desperate one by most standards – the desert. In the book of Exodus, we find Moses, the former adopted son of the Pharaoh, now in exile in the desert. He killed an Egyptian who was beating a fellow Israelite slave. When he heard Pharaoh wanted to kill him in response, Moses ran away in fear (Exodus 2:11-15).

Fast forward forty years and we find Moses still in the desert, this time talking to God Who appeared to him in a burning bush (Exodus 3). When God told Moses He was going use him to deliver His people from the bonds of Egyptian slavery, Moses was again gripped with fear. He made excuses about why he should not take on that role, despite the fact that God assured him He would be with him everywhere Moses went. Moses feared no one would listen to or follow him. He feared they would remember he killed a man and assumed Pharaoh still wanted to kill him.

Succumbing to this fear would have left Moses in the desert for life and the nation of Israel in bondage. We know Moses finally accepted God's assignment despite his fears, and God used him to lead the Israelites out of Egyptian bondage.

Another very interesting and impactful *fear* story involved Moses and the entire nation of Israel. Most people know the Jews wandered around in the desert for forty years after leaving Egypt. Most do not know why. It was their choice. They chose *fear* and God chose to let them wander forty years as a reminder.

You can read the full story in Numbers 13. The trip to the Promised Land was a relatively short one from Egypt. When that mass of people arrived in the area, Moses sent twelve spies to check it out. Two of them, Joshua and Caleb, returned and talked about how great it was and ready for the taking. But the other ten warned that the land was filled with giants, and said death loomed if they tried to go into this Promised Land.

Who did Moses and the entire nation listen to? Even though they had recently seen God part the Red Sea to deliver them from the Egyptians, they listened to the ten and not the two. That decision, based solely on fear, so angered God that He sentenced all those who were alive to die in the desert. He spared only the families of Joshua and Caleb. So they wandered in the desert for forty years while the unbelievers died out.

God is a rewarder of faith, not fear.

Fear often leads men into desperate places. It causes us to stay put when we should be going forward or make wrong turns that take us into places that heighten rather than assuage fear.

Anger. This is one of those problems that usually creates as much self-inflicted damage as it does collateral damage. That was certainly the case with Joe Jr. His anger toward his father eventually led him into a life of crime of his own, which, as we know, landed him in prison alongside his dad. Nothing could have made him madder. God uses strange means to get our attention and teach lessons we otherwise would not learn. Even with that, there is no guarantee we learn them.

The first murder in history occurred when Cain killed his brother, Abel. The motive? Anger. This always seemed to me one of the oddest Bible stories and hard to understand. Cain was a farmer and Abel a shepherd. Both men offered sacrifices to God. We read in Genesis 4 that God accepted Abel's offering of the fat of sheep but rejected the fruit offered by Cain. Angry, jealous, and feeling rejected, Cain lured Abel into a field and killed him without cause.

Anger is a natural emotion and can have it's place. But throughout the Bible, and even in our lives, we read and see firsthand that anger is the precursor of many sins and issues. Bitterness. Envy. Jealousy. Revenge.

Failure to manage our anger becomes a road that leads men into desperate places with potentially the worst consequences of all as we saw in the lives of Joe Jr. and Cain, many thousands of years apart.

Pride. It is not a stretch to say that *pride* killed Charles' father. He took his own life, but that singular act was the result of a deadly combination—the collapse of his god (money) and a pride that was shattered as a result. When Charles became a man, he walked very much in his father's shoes. His pursuit to restore the family status and wealth became his consuming passion at the expense of his relationships with his wife and children. He failed to realize he was not *building wealth for his family*, he was *building walls between them and himself*.

One example of a prideful man in the Bible is the story of Naaman found in 2 Kings 5:1-14. Naaman was captain of the king's army and highly respected. He was also a leper. As I did initially, you may think it is odd to link pride with a leper. However his story reveals that, despite his disease, he was a man of immense pride.

Naaman's story began when a Jewish slave girl who served his wife suggested he go to "the man of God" for healing. After some political pandering between kings, he ended up on the doorstep of Elisha. Naaman and his party waited outside for the man of God to come out to greet him. Instead, Elisha sent his servant out with instructions for him to follow if he wanted to be healed:

"Go wash in the Jordan River seven times and your flesh will be restored and you will be clean."

Naaman was furious at such a suggestion. He was an important captain of the army and sent by his king. His response exposes his pride:

"Are not the rivers of Damascus better than all the waters of Israel? Could I not wash in them and be clean?"

So Naaman went away angry, full of pride, and still a leper. Fortunately, his servants talked some sense (humility) into him. Naaman recanted his prideful position and followed Elisha's instructions. He dipped seven times in the Jordan River. Immediately he was healed.

The Bible offers many warnings about the consequences of taking the road of pride. Perhaps the best and most appropriate for our discussion are these words of Solomon.

"Pride goes before destruction, a haughty spirit before a fall."
                                              Proverbs 16: 18 NIV

Pride is the road that leads some men to their end as we saw in the case of Charles' father. While that end is the most extreme, pride often blinds men from seeing the truth. And blind men should not be driving on any road, especially this one.

Temptation. It would be more accurate to use "yielding to temptation" as the heading. Temptation is not sin. After all, Jesus was tempted for forty days in the desert by Satan. He did not yield to any of them, rather rebuking Satan by quoting Scripture each time he threw another one at Him.

Thomas, even though he was a pastor, was certainly not immune to temptation. In his case, temptation overtook him and the secret sin of pornography enslaved him. Had he inadvertently come across that porn site while preparing his paper and immediately moved on or blocked the site, his life would have been very different. Yet he hung around too long, enticed by the visual pleasure and stimulation, and that choice eventually cost him his ministry and, more importantly, his family.

Since we find the first temptation of man near the very beginning of the Bible (Genesis 3), Adam is an obvious choice as the biblical counterpart to Pastor Thomas. Adam and Eve were given their operating instructions and one ground rule. Do not eat the fruit of just one tree.

You know the story. Along came the most cunning and crafty creature, the serpent, to make Eve an offer she could not refuse. (And you thought that originated with the Godfather!) Eve was seduced by the serpent and what he offered. So she caved in and ate the forbidden fruit. Then she persuaded Adam to eat. And the rest, as they say, is history.

Every man who has ever lived has been tempted in many ways. We find temptations on every road and at every turn. Some are subtle in nature, while others are much larger in scale and offer greater reward for the risk.

This road finds temptations surfacing when we least expect them or showing up at every turn. The shoulders of this temptation road are littered with wrecked lives of men who yielded to them or pulled over to check them out and stayed just one minute too long.

Lust. The Bible states there are three types of sin common to man and two are positioned as forms of lust.

> *"For all that is in the world, the* **lust of the flesh** *and the* **lust of the eyes** *and the* **boastful pride of life***, is not from the Father, but is from the world."*
> 1 John 2: 16 NASB

Lust of the flesh is self-explanatory. It is most often connected to sexual sins, like adultery. *Lust of the eyes* is coveting what you don't have, or what belongs to someone else. And we discussed the sin of pride earlier in this chapter.

David, our sales executive friend, fell victim to all three. His workaholism was a form of pride that led to him being away from his wife and family too much. The sins of lust sins are more obvious and manifest themselves in ways that create victims on both sides. David, his associate, his wife and kids.

We left David in a very desperate place with a tough decision to make. Confess the adultery and deal with the fallout from the consequences or try to hide it. Such things are never easy to hide as guilt has a way of bubbling up to the surface and being exposed.

I gave the name *David* to our businessman friend because I knew I was going to use King David, the man after God's own heart, as the biblical counterpart in this section on *lust*. Bible stories about David are some of the best known of all. The young shepherd who killed large animals protecting his father's sheep. The young warrior who killed Goliath to protect his Father's people. His saga to become king that took years. But the best-known story of all is that of David and Bathsheba. It is the kind Hollywood people like because it is full of lust, adultery, and murder. You can read their story in 2 Samuel 3.

You may recall David was strolling around on the palace roof, perhaps admiring his kingdom, when he glanced across the rooftops and his eyes were pierced with a most beautiful sight. Across the way, Bathsheba, a married woman, was bathing on her rooftop. Overcome with lust, King David wasted no time having Bathsheba brought to his palace. And it was not to ask her opinion on kingdom matters.

That set off a series of events that led to the downfall of David's family. For example, we know King Solomon, David's son, had hundreds of wives and concubines in his palace even though he knew God did not approve. Ultimately the kingdom split in half with two kings and was never again reunited before both fell captive to the enemies. No more nation of Israel for thousands of years. It began with lust fulfilled.

Sadly, I imagine you have friends who also went down this path. Perhaps this is part of your story. Some end with confession, forgiveness, and redemption. But more often, those marriages end up as carnage along the roadside.

We have considered five different roads that lead men into desperate places. One common denominator is that all five roads lead men to make bad decisions. And those bad decisions have been known to keep us in desperate places. For example,

- *Fear* paralyzes men.
- *Anger* makes men irrational.
- *Pride* causes men to think our way is always best.

- *Temptations* entice men to make decisions based on feelings alone.
- *Lust* enslaves men and holds us captive.

Sooner or later even the most stubborn men hit the wall and come to the end of themselves. That endpoint leaves us with another decision to make.

- Do I remain in my desperate place and continue to deal with the consequences of my bad decisions?
- Do I try to find a road that leads me out of here?

For men who choose the latter, I suggest there are only two roads out. Neither is a *freeway* like most roads we travel. Quite the opposite. Both of these roads out of desperate places come at great cost. We know them as *toll roads*.

Questions Every Desperate Man Needs to Answer

1) Fear. *"Fear causes men to stay put when we should be going forward or make wrong turns that take us into places that heighten rather than assuage fear."* What are some of the sources of fear that hold or paralyze men and keep us from moving forward? Conversely, what are some other sources or kinds of fear that cause men to run away?

2) Anger. *"Failure to manage our anger becomes a road into desperate places with potentially the worst consequences of all…"* What causes a man to get so angry that he would murder another man as Cain did? What are some of the other consequences of anger that were mentioned in the chapter? What are some things that push your anger "hot button?"

3) Pride. Naaman was a leper whose pride was easily offended, which seems ironic. Yet we are all men with spiritual issues akin to his physical ones. What are some areas of pride that lead men to desperate places or even destruction (as Proverbs teaches)? What areas in your life have been built by walls of pride, like those of Charles' father? What are you doing to tear them down before they tear you down?

4) Temptation. The problem is not temptation. All men are tempted – even Jesus. The problem is yielding (giving in) to it. Temptations come in many sizes and shapes and from many

areas of life. What areas of temptation are common to men regardless of whether or not a man is a Christian? What areas plague you the most? What do you do to keep from yielding?

5) Lust. "*Lust* enslaves men and holds us captive." The Bible teaches that lust comes in two varieties: *the lust of the flesh* and *the lust of the eyes*. What is the difference? Give some examples of each type. Which ones do you struggle with most?

Personal Reflections on My Journey:

CHAPTER FIVE

Toll Roads – The Only Way Out

To this point, we spent considerable time examining what desperate men look like and the roads that facilitate our journeys into desperate places. Once there, few men are comfortable or content to remain there. The pain associated with the consequences of our bad decisions makes us naturally want out. Most of us begin almost immediately looking for a way out.

While this may fall in the "life is not fair" category, we know there are at least five roads that lead in, yet I suggest there are only two roads out. To make matters worse, both are *toll roads*.

I imagine all of us have taken toll roads from one point to another during the course of driving around the country. On most, we do not pay to get on but we have to pay to get off. The farther we travel, the more it costs. The same may be said of the two toll roads that get us out of desperate places. I should add two similarities exist between both:
1. Someone must pay the toll.
2. As we will see, both end up at the same place.

One huge difference exists between them that demands our attention and discussion.

> *The first toll road comes at great cost to men;*
> *the second at great cost to God.*

Toll Road #1: My Way

We are by nature highly self-sufficient and proud of it. We like to do and have things our way. I feel certain that was the origin of the expression, "*my way or the highway.*"

Throughout biblical history, the self-sufficiency of men led them to choose the "My Way" toll road. Those decisions often extracted a high cost and was accompanied by great loss. Like many of us, our ancestors had little trouble finding their ways into desperate places via this path. Consider these examples:

- Adam went off-roading in the bushes to hide from God. (ref. Genesis 3: 8)
- Abraham took a short cut to an heir. Tired of waiting on God for the promised son, he sired Ishmael, a decision that has haunted Israel throughout its history. (ref. Genesis 16: 2-4)
- David's bumpiest of roads led to adultery, death, murder, and a very dysfunctional family. (ref. 2 Samuel 11-13, 18)
- Jonah saw the road God had for him and ran in the other direction. (ref. Jonah 1: 1-3)
- The rich young ruler turned and walked away from Jesus, preferring the one he was on to the one Jesus suggested. (ref. Matthew 19: 16-22)
- Saul thought he was on the right road to persecute more Christians until Jesus showed up and blocked his path. (ref. Acts 9)

We have several things in common with these ancient biblical brethren. First, all of us have a propensity to choose our own way that seems right to us.

Second, the ways we choose often turn out to be very costly, eerily similar to the ones our forefathers took. They lead to severed marriages, broken homes, insecure children, men hiding secret sins and enslaved by addictions of every kind, worshipping gods of position, wealth and power. God has much to say about men who choose any or all of those "my way" paths. Here is one example.

> *"I permitted Myself to be sought by those who did not ask for Me; I permitted Myself to be found by those who did not seek Me. I said, 'Here am I, here am I,' to a nation which did not call on My name. I have spread out My hands all day long to a rebellious people, Who walk in the **way** which is not good, **following their own thoughts.**"*
> Isaiah 65: 1-2 NASB

This paints a picture of God jumping up and down waving His arms. "Here I am. Listen to Me!" God offered the way out, but men chose to follow their own thoughts and ways. Many still do. If He used one of the more popular rhetorical questions today, God would ask such men, *"How's that working for you?"*

This cry of God to desperate men in all places and every walk of life provides a great segue to the second toll road. ***God's Way.***

Toll Road #2: God's Way.

> *"A highway will be there, a roadway. And it will be called the Highway of Holiness."*
> Isaiah 35:8 NASB

Long before God spoke these words to His people through the prophet Isaiah, He called Abram out of his homeland, Ur. That is modern day Iraq. The writer of Hebrews told us that, in faith, "Abraham went out not knowing where he was going." God put him on what would become Abram's *highway to holiness,* not one of his own choosing.

God told Abram he would become the father and leader of a great nation with descendants too numerous to count. God also changed his name to Abraham. Abram was seventy-five years old when this promise was made. Sarai his wife was 66 (Genesis 15).

Fast forward twenty-four years, and again we find God speaking to Abraham to confirm the promise of an heir from his own flesh. Abraham laughed as he asked God if a son could be born to a 100-year-old man and a ninety-year-old wife (Genesis 17). But the joke was on Abraham and Sarah. Isaac was born one year later just as God promised twenty-five years earlier. One lesson learned from this part of the story is God is patient when we are not.

The faithfulness of God and trustworthiness of His promises continue to be demonstrated to Abraham and Sarah in Genesis 22. God instructed Abraham to take Isaac and sacrifice him as a burnt offering. That would seem preposterous to us on every front. It was a pagan practice. Abraham had waited twenty-five years for the birth of Isaac. Now God told him to willingly kill him? Shockingly, Abraham offered no rebuttal, which must speak volumes about his faith, perhaps learned over that twenty-five year waiting period.

Abraham trusted God enough to obey this incredible command. He believed God would someone how make it right because of the covenant promise God made that his descendants would be "too numerous to count." When Isaac asked about not having a sheep to sacrifice, Abraham answered, "God will provide the sacrifice." Another great statement of faith.

Only when Abraham raised his knife to kill Isaac did God intervene. He told him to stop. Abraham looked around, and there he saw a ram caught in a thicket. Just as He promised and with no help or input from Abraham (or Isaac), God provided the sacrifice. Abraham demonstrated great faith. God demonstrated His all-sufficiency. (Genesis 22: 1-19)

This amazing story illustrates the second *toll road* out of desperate places, *God's Way*. It was made possible by His unconditional love, built on His mercy, and paved by His grace.

I want to close this section of the book with good news. For men who chose the *my way* toll road, I want you to know there is still hope. No matter how circuitous, difficult, disgusting, or sinful the toll road or toll roads you took to escape your desperate places, know this:

> ***All roads ultimately lead to the same place...***
> ***the foot of the Cross of Christ.***

But, my dear friend, it is not enough to simply come to the foot of the cross. Desperate men must be willing to hear, understand, and receive its Message, Jesus. Part Two of *Desperate Men* is devoted to helping desperate men move from a place of *observation* in front of the Cross to the place of *obedience* on the other side that God intended for you. I refer to that process as *The Journey through the Cross*.

Questions Every Desperate Man Needs to Answer

"There are only two roads that lead men out of desperate places. Both are toll roads. My Way and God's Way."

1) It may seem a "no-brainer" to ask this, but which one is better? _____ If God's way is the clear and obvious choice, why do men spend so much time trying to build our own roads out?

2) What are some of the more typical roads men choose that often lead into even more desperate places?

3) What lessons can we learn from Abraham's journey?

Personal Reflections on My Journey:

PART TWO

The Journey *Through* the Cross

This pivotal section of the book was written for desperate men who would comfortably or uncomfortably check one of the following boxes to describe their relationship with God:

- ☐ I do not have one. I have never accepted Christ as my personal Savior.

- ☐ I think I am a Christian, but I am not exactly sure what you mean by that.

- ☐ I have received Christ as my Savior but there is no evidence or fruit in my life.

- ☐ I am a biblical Christian striving to live under the power and guidance of the Holy Spirit, knowing I am still a work in progress.

Regardless of what place in life you find yourself relationally toward God today, I want you to know there is meat inside this section for you to chew on. By the time you finish this journey through the Cross of Christ:

- ☑ You will understand your desperate place and need for a Savior. You will be encouraged and challenged to receive God's gift of amazing grace now.
- ☑ Any confusion about what it means to be a *biblical* Christian versus a *cultural* one will be cleared up. Then you can answer life's most important question with assurance.

- ☑ The process God uses to build men does not stop with our salvation … it begins there. On the other side of the cross you will learn that power to live is found only in the Holy Spirit.

- ☑ My dear brother in Christ, on the other side of the cross you will either be reminded or shown what it looks like to live desperately for God from this point forward.

Let's begin this journey through the cross with expectation that God has something inside with your name on it; something written to and for you through the awesome inspiration of His Spirit. My prayer is whatever that is, you will pick it up and make it your own. Let's head to the courtroom.

CHAPTER SIX

Two Trials, One Verdict

We begin this part of our journey by quietly peeking behind the veil of time into the past. Picture yourself sitting high in the back of the courtroom balcony as you watch and listen in.

The Trial of Mankind

The courtroom was packed that day, the gallery filled with every heavenly being and fallen angel that managed to work its way into the room. All of creation waited anxiously for the trial of mankind to begin. The outcome would have far-reaching, eternal ramifications.

A sole defendant entered the courtroom unescorted. I could not believe my eyes. He was Jesus, the Son of God. How could He be on trial for the sins of mankind? He must have chosen to defend Himself, because He sat quietly alone at the defendant's table.

Across the aisle sat the prosecutor, Satan himself, clothed in hate and overflowing with contempt. How could this fallen angel, who rebelled against God and was cast out of Heaven, be the prosecutor of all men? Was this some kind of a mock trial? Surely this case would be thrown out for lack of merit.

Suddenly a hush fell over the courtroom extending across the whole universe. The archangel Gabriel entered the room trumpeting the arrival of the Judge. Every living being and all of creation bowed low as God Almighty entered the courtroom. He took His place behind the bench, called the trial to order, and turned the proceedings over to Satan, the prosecutor.

Satan took center stage and began his opening argument. With venomous words befitting a serpent, he attacked mankind for its weak and sinful ways. He began with father Adam and proceeded to march through human history, indicting one sinful man after another.

He went especially hard after David, later called "the man after God's own heart," citing his weak, pathetic successors. Jesus Messiah, the Savior of the world, would come from that dysfunctional family? It was full of sinners and weak men, even a prostitute. Brazenly, Satan challenged the virginity of Mary, mother of Jesus, attempting to disqualify her as well. Satan was vicious and relentless in his attacks on the weakness of man and sinfulness of mankind.

When he completed this tirade of an opening argument, he called only one witness—Jesus. Salivating with hatred and indignation, Satan lashed out at Him. "How can You defend this pathetic human race"? He laughed cynically as he questioned Jesus about His motley band of followers, one of whom betrayed Him as the others who ran away. Men would not stand with Him. Why should He stand for them?

Satan paused, waiting on Jesus to respond. Every heavenly being in the gallery and all of creation leaned in with great anticipation to hear what Jesus would say. Surely He would come to the defense of man. He would overwhelm Satan with His eloquent words and strong defense. Every demonic creature cowered, fearing their time would soon be over.

Much to their shock and surprise, Jesus remained silent. Satan repeated his claims with even more fervor. Still Jesus offered no defense. Satan rested his case.

In a brief closing argument, Satan called attention to the fact that Jesus offered no excuses or rebuttal for the sins of mankind. The trial portion ended nearly as quickly as it began. Since there was no jury, there were no long deliberations. All of creation waited anxiously for the verdict to be pronounced.

The great Judge, Jehovah God, had no choice but to find mankind guilty of sin as charged. The verdict pronounced, Satan raised his arms in victory as every demon throughout the universe cheered this great victory. Now all that remained was the sentencing phase. The sentence came down swiftly and harshly. All of mankind was sentenced to death.

Wailing and weeping filled the air as heavenly beings and all of creation moaned the death penalty. The demonic realm cheered wildly. This meant they would enjoy victory over all of mankind throughout history. And when God brought the world to an end, mankind would be dragged along with them into the eternal place of suffering Jesus called Hell.

Then amidst the tears and cheers, the most amazing thing happened. Jesus rose to His feet. The Son of God and man, silent throughout the trial offering no defense, spoke words no one could believe or would ever forget: ***"I will die in their place."***

The entire courtroom and all of creation were stunned by Jesus' words. Never before nor ever since would there be such a demonstration of unconditional love and sacrifice. And for such a guilty and undeserving race – mankind. Jesus' words broke the very heart of God, for He knew how this would play out at a future time. Satan fell back in his chair. The hate that had filled his eyes now turned to fear.

With tears in His eyes, the great Judge, Jehovah God, accepted the terms of Jesus' offer. Jesus would be executed for the sins of mankind at a time and place to be designated. He closed the trial with three words, "It is finishedd"—words that would come back to haunt Satan and all who followed him.

The stage was set for Jesus the Messiah to enter human history at the appointed time. All biblical prophecy, written across thousands of years of Old Testament history from Genesis to Malachi, would be fulfilled.

The Trial for *Your* Life

Fast-forward through history to the present day. We enter another courtroom where a trial is about to begin. Yours. You are on trial for your life. And as in the trial of eternity past, God presides as Judge and Jury; Satan is your prosecutorial accuser.

The Charges

What an odd scene. God asks what charges are brought against you. Satan rises and begins to read from the Bible using the Word of God to accuse you. "I did not see that coming," you think to yourself. Satan reads only two verses in his opening argument, both written by the Apostle Paul, himself a former accuser of Christians:

> *"For all have sinned and fall short of the glory of God."* Romans 3:23 NASB

> *"For the wages of sin is death..."* Romans 6:23 NASB

Throughout your life, the Holy Spirit of God tried to convince and convict you of the need to confess and accept Jesus, Who died for the sins of mankind, a penalty agreed upon in eternity past. That simple act of humility and obedience on your part would have set aside all charges against you. But you felt good enough about your position in life and standing with God. So you refused to heed His warnings and take your chances. You took the "my way" toll road and lived your life on your own terms. Regrettable.

For really stupid reasons that seemed smart at the time, you chose to defend yourself at this trial. That happens a lot with men. It makes Satan, your accuser, chuckle. You trusted in your own skills and ability to talk your way out of just about anything. You have an amazing ability to rationalize away all of your shortcomings and have done so your whole life. Now we will see how that works for you as you stand before almighty, holy God with your life hanging in the balance.

Witnesses for the Prosecution

Satan begins to call witnesses against you. He calls family, friends, and business associates. One by one, they speak of good and bad things you did throughout your life. Satan drills down on the bad things you said or did. Now they flash before your eyes like a neon sign. In the end, most people say you were a "good man." The question is *were you good enough?* Unfortunately, as you are about to learn, that does not matter. It is not about being good enough. It is about being perfect and holy like God.

The Defensive Defense

Now it is your turn to take the witness stand. Prior to this, you feel certain you can stand before God, turn on the charm, and articulate all the good in your life. He is a loving God, after all, and merciful too. Surely He would give you a pass. Worried, shaken, and wishing you had an experienced trial lawyer on your side, you walk slowly to the stand. You prepared five lines of defense thinking one of them would surely get you acquitted. Now you are not so certain.

Defense #1: "It's not my fault."

Blame remains atop the list of most men when our lives are subject to cross-examination, and you are no exception. You argue someone else caused you to do the wrong thing, make the wrong choice, or turn down the wrong road. In fact, you are the real victim.

This is a tough line of defense and hardly original. Perhaps you did not know or you forgot that Adam threw Eve under the bus, blaming her for the very first sin. *"That woman you gave to be with me made me eat…"* Eve turned around and blamed the serpent. God was unpersuaded by both arguments as demonstrated by the sentences He handed down (Genesis 3:12). Next argument.

Defense #2: "That's not fair.
Most kids grow up using that phrase. As parents, we grow weary of hearing it as we explain, in fact, life is not fair. Part of growing up and maturing is learning to deal with it. Continuing to use that excuse as a grown man is unacceptable. You still feel like you have been mistreated and life owes you something. It does not. Look at Job. Would you say life treated him fairly? Has your life been as hard as his? (Job 1:6-22.) Next argument.

Defense #3: "I have lived a good life."
Compared to whom? Billy Graham? Mother Teresa? A criminal or thief? How are you defining a "good life?" Someone who obeys most of the laws? Helps little old ladies across the street? Puts money in the plate at church every Easter? Tries to be a good neighbor and co-worker?

I have bad news for you: Good works, no matter how many or how good, cannot save you or get your case dismissed. The Apostle Paul learned this and wrote about it on several occasions.
Here is one example:

> *"He saved us, not on the basis of deeds which we have done in righteousness, but according to His mercy, by the washing of regeneration and renewing by the Holy Spirit."* Titus 3:5, NASB

There is only one good life that was ever lived according to God's scale of *good*. The perfect life of Christ. Have you lived a perfect life? Of course not. Next argument.

Defense #4: "I am not as bad as they are."
The "Theory of Relativity" as men apply it in their defense is a popular one. We measure the number or severity of our sins against those of others. You contrast yourself with murderers, thieves, other bad people, and argue you never did such horrible things. They were bad guys and you are good in comparison. That should be enough to get you into Heaven, if there is one.

Feeble attempt. Jesus taught "*sin is sin*" in the Sermon on the Mount (Matthew 5:21-48). There are no "good guys" in Heaven and "bad guys" in Hell, just men who refused to accept God's terms of salvation and forgiveness. Any more arguments?

Defense #5: "No one is perfect!"
You are right. That is the point. All men are guilty. There is not one "good" man among the lot. You offer every form of excuse man can conceive. All sorely lack veracity, and more importantly, God remains unpersuaded. The real truth of this matter is *"…men are without excuse."* (Romans 1: 20 NASB) Herein lies the problem. Jesus said, *"Be perfect as I am perfect"* (Matthew 5:48 NASB). How can a man be perfect? We can't. No man is or will be perfect, but you can be *made perfect*. Big difference.

Uncomfortably, you rest your defense.

The Verdict: You stand and God renders the only verdict possible. Guilty. Satan smiles with delight. He knew this was the only possible outcome. Sin makes all men guilty. Man cannot do enough good works, live a perfect life, or come up with any acceptable excuse to bring a verdict of innocent.

The Sentence. As it was in the trial of mankind, the sentence is again the death penalty. Your worst nightmare becomes reality. You find this hard to believe, but that is not the worst part. This death penalty is not physical in nature. All men die at some point. Instead, this sentence refers to *spiritual* death. The sentence served out in Hell for the balance of eternity. You quickly filed an appeal. This will be your last chance to escape the death penalty.

Questions Every Desperate Man Needs to Answer

1) What created the need for the Trial of Mankind?

2) Why was Jesus the defendant?

3) Why couldn't God find Jesus, His own Son, innocent because He had not sinned?

4) If Jesus stood trial for the sins of mankind, why do we have to stand trial?

5) The five excuses men use most were discussed. Which one(s) have you used? Can you think of others?

Personal Reflections on My Journey:

CHAPTER SEVEN

Your Final Appeal

Every condemned man has the right to appeal his verdict. However, in this case you have a hard road ahead. No higher authority exists to whom you can argue your case. Knowing this is your last shot, you devise a strategy you believe is sure to move God to set aside the verdict and stay your sentence. (Desperate men are known to come up with incredible arguments to justify their actions and save their necks, some of which we already heard.)

Until now your best excuses and arguments have neither moved the hand nor the heart of God. For your final appeal, you decide to try to outsmart God by putting Him on the spot with one question:

> *"If You are good and love all people like You say You do, why would You sentence anyone to eternity in Hell just because he rejects Christ as the only way to have his sins forgiven? There must be other ways!"*

You could not have asked a better question. Whether you knew it or not, this question sits atop the list of every condemned or unbelieving person in the world who refuses to surrender and submit to God through Christ alone. "That just does not seem right. It seems narrow minded and bigoted, exclusive rather than inclusive." Those are but a few of the arguments used by many who have gone before you as well as some of your contemporaries.

You place your final hope in throwing the *love* and *goodness* of God back in His face, hoping He will reconsider such harsh judgment. Over the centuries, millions of others have offered the same arguments.

The answer to that questions resides in a full understanding of who God is – what He reveals about His nature and personality to us through the Bible. For example, we know that God is holy, loving, patient, and merciful. He graciously offers us an opportunity know Him and the expressions of His love, even though we do not deserve it because of our sins.

But there are other parts of His character, each of which are just as much a part of His nature as the others. God is righteous. He is perfect. He is wrathful because of His hatred of sin. He is just and demands justice on His terms alone. No one attribute is greater in force or effect than another.

That presents a real problem to many people. They do not like to think of God's wrath and judgment, so they ignore it. That is a big part of this problem. You cannot "cherry pick" those things you like about God or the ones you think are "fair."

People like it that God is love, full of grace and mercy, and altogether good. That is absolutely true. And as much as God is love, full of grace and mercy, and good, He is also holy, righteous, just, and "wrathful." That language gives a lot of people serious heartburn. But it is as much a part of God as love. He said so in the Bible.

Wrap your mind around this. The Bible contains more references to the anger and wrath of God than His love and mercy. Most people do not like that. So they ignore it or cut those verses from their Bibles.

But that is not what God intended. God intends for us to take Him at His Word, all of it—even if don't like it or agree with it.

I hope this provides some insight into God our Father and His amazing, long-suffering love for us. We will come back to this shortly. Let's return to the appeal hearing to get the final ruling.

The Verdict

You give it your best shot. You argue eloquently and passionately until your voice gives out. You even plead for a lighter sentence; anything but death. But in the end, good works and good behavior are not part of God's equation for salvation. Blood alone provides the only acceptable covering for the sins of man. And that requires death. After patiently listening to your earnest pleas, God simply says, *"Appeal denied."*

Desperate man, indeed. What will happen now? Faced with certain death and completely desperate for a way to mitigate your sentence, there is nowhere left to turn.

Though these proceedings are imaginary, the trials are very real. When your turn comes—and it will—many of you will find yourselves presenting the same excuses and the same final appeal.

But I want you to know there is hope. Beyond your failed appeal, God made a way.

Recall as *the trial of mankind* came to a close, Jesus volunteered to take the place of mankind and die for our sins. At the appointed time in history, Jesus became *the sacrificial Lamb of God.* His death (shed blood) brought life through forgiveness of sins for all who would believe. He was the only perfect sacrifice, once for all.

We began this chapter at the foot of the Cross upon which Jesus' death sentence (crucifixion) was executed. We took on some hard questions, some of which have harder answers, unpopular with many today who oppose conservative biblical Christian precepts. Unconditional love that begs obedience. Grace and mercy found only in Christ. Death penalties. A better understanding of the complete nature of God. I am grateful if you hung in there with me to this point because these are points on which many men fall away.

As I wrote when we began this part of our journey, my objective is to move men standing in front of the Cross through the Cross where God awaits with our final assignment. To do so requires drilling down in the final well that reaches the oil of God's lamp and produces "gushers" in the hearts of men brave enough to let it cover over them. *The Meaning and Message of the Cross.*

Questions Every Desperate Man Needs to Answer

1) *"If You (God) are good and love all people like You say You do, why would You sentence anyone to eternity in Hell just because he rejects Christ as the only way to have his sins forgiven? There must be other ways!"*

    How do you respond to that question? _____
    _____
    _____

2) If you were standing before God and given the chance to appeal your "guilty" verdict, what would you say in your own defense?
    _____
    _____
    _____

Personal Reflections on My Journey:
_____
_____
_____
_____

CHAPTER EIGHT

The Desperation of God
The Meaning and Message of the Cross

Not far outside the city walls of Jerusalem a man and his son walked along a road that led past a gloomy-looking hill. The son paused and stared at the hill for a minute. "Papa, that place scares me," he said to his father. "It's creepy. It looks like a man's skull. What are those wooden things sticking out on top?"

The boy's father replied, "That hill is Golgotha. It means 'skull.' Some say it is called that because it resembles a skull."

"What do they do up there?"

"Those wooden things you see sticking out of the ground are crosses," the father said.

Naturally the curious son asked, "What are crosses for?"

"They use them to crucify bad men." The father grew more uncomfortable as the conversation proceeded.

Of course the anxious son asked the one question the father didn't want to answer, "What is crucifixion?" As gently as he could, the father explained what many consider the most gruesome process mankind ever created for executing the death penalty.

In the time of Christ, crucifixion was a means of capital punishment. So a cross projected three meanings that all the people understood: *suffering, public humiliation,* and *death.*

Suffering. At every turn during the trial and His preparation for execution, Jesus was beaten and abused in unimaginable ways. Soldiers spat in His face. They mocked and laughed at Him. The intent of the Romans was to make a condemned man feel completely worthless and deserving of death.

In Jesus' case, soldiers took particular delight in fabricating a wreath of thorns and forcing it into his skull as a crown. The pain was excruciating as intended. Then they forced him to carry His cross up the hill to His place of execution. You may recall Jesus was so weakened by the beating and abuse He could not continue to carry His cross. The Romans picked a man out of the crowd to do so. Then the death squad and "criminal" proceeded to the place of execution.

Public humiliation. The Romans wanted all people under their rule to observe firsthand in horror what happened to those who dared to oppose them. The public could watch as the criminals were brutally nailed to their crosses. Spikes, large enough to penetrate flesh and bone into a large wooden beam, were driven with great force by the soldiers. Onlookers watched in terror, while others walked on by, thinking the person must be getting his just punishment. After all, they only crucified really bad people, right?

The practice that amazes me as much or perhaps more than people watching public executions is that of mocking and taunting the dying men. We know from Scripture that soldiers mocked Jesus throughout the time before and after His trials. Then on the cross, fellow Jews taunted Him, demanding He come down to prove He was Messiah.

Death. When people of Jesus' time saw a cross, it meant one thing: someone was going to die. Not just be punished or tortured for a while, but put to death. There was no way of escape. The guilty one could not appeal at this point, nor could he repent and admit guilt, hoping for a lesser penalty.

For Christians, the Cross bears another more significant meaning. We agree the cross was an instrument of physical death. But in the case of Jesus Christ, it was death that would produce life for all believers throughout history.

Beyond the meaning of the Cross, Christians believe the *message of the Cross* speaks so loudly every man must hear it, though not all will believe. Here are five of those messages that God conveyed to men through the Cross of Christ.

☦ **The Cross cleared a way out of desperate places.** We closed the previous chapter with the analogy that God paid the toll for man out of desperate places with the blood of Christ. God turned an impassable toll road into a freeway to the cross. The Apostle Paul articulated this message as follows:

> *"When you were dead in your transgressions and the uncircumcision of your flesh, He made you alive together with Him, having forgiven us all our transgressions, having canceled out the certificate of debt consisting of decrees against us, which was hostile to us; and He has taken it (sin) out of the way, having nailed it to the cross.*   Colossians 2:13-14 NASB

☦ **The Cross confronts men with the Truth.** The historical reality of the cross is not disputed by most historians. The Apostle Paul directly confronted men with the truth of the gospel referring to the Cross of Christ.

> *"For Christ did not send me to baptize, but to preach the gospel, not in cleverness of speech, so that the Cross of Christ would not*

be made void. For the word of the cross is foolishness to those who are perishing, but to us who are being saved it is the power of God."
1 Corinthians 1:17-18 NASB

In that same passage, Paul called the cross a "stumbling block" to the Jews. By this, he meant they were expecting a different kind of Messiah, a king or mighty ruler, not a poor man from Nazareth who died a miserable death. They could not digest the truth of the Cross of Christ.

✝ **The Cross convicts men.** The Cross of Christ not only *confronts* men, it also *convicts* men of our sin. As we covered previously, the only reason the need for the cross existed was our sin that bore the death penalty. Sin entered into the human race by man and it could only be removed by the One the Apostle Paul refers to as "the last Adam" (1 Corinthians 15:45). The last Adam was God incarnate, Jesus, the Man who lived a perfect life enabling Him to be a worthy sacrifice.

Jesus' spoke of this in His own words. First He gave us His mission statement. Then He told us why He was sending the Holy Spirit after He ascended into Heaven. The message is clear.

"I have not come to call the righteous but sinners to repentance."
Luke 5:32 NASB

"And He, when He (the Holy Spirit) comes, will convict the world concerning sin and righteousness and judgment." John 16:8 NASB

✝ **The Cross calls men to follow Him out of desperate places.** Like a flashing arrow pointing the way to a weary traveler on a dark night, or a lighthouse beacon penetrating the rain and fog to guide a wayward ship safely into port, the Cross of Christ calls lost men, desperate for a Savior. Jesus uses three metaphors to call men to Himself.

He is the Light of the World. *"Jesus again spoke to them, saying, "I am the Light of the world; he who follows Me will not walk in the darkness, but will have the Light of life."* John 8:12 NASB

He is the Open Door. *"I am the door; if anyone enters through Me, he will be saved, and will go in and out and find pasture."* John 10:9 NASB

He is the Good Shepherd. *"I am the good shepherd and the good shepherd lays down his life for the sheep.* John 10:11 NASB

☦ **The Cross creates a crisis of decision.**
The sum of those four messages of the Cross creates an urgent message no man can ignore. They present a case so strong, we must confront them as truth or forever deal with the consequences.

When I was a child I watched a television game, *Truth or Consequences*. The contestant had to make the correct decision (tell the truth) or they would suffer the consequences (be part of various funny stunts or pratfalls).

Unfortunately life is not a game show we can turn on or off. Life is a continuum of decisions, all of which bear consequences, some good, others not so much. The meaning and messages of the Cross of Christ demand a decision from all men. For a number of reasons, we make this decision harder than it is.

My friend, please consider this carefully.

Either Jesus was just:
– *a good man who*
– *was a spellbinding communicator claiming to be the Son of God and Messiah and*
– *performed mystifying "miracles" like a magician but*
– *died a horrible death for nothing. End of story. What a shame.*

OR
Jesus was:
- Who He said He was, Messiah, God Incarnate, the Son of God,
- Who fulfilled hundreds of prophecies dating back thousands of years,
- Accepted the "death penalty" for the sins of mankind, once and for all, on the Cross and
- Rose again, defeating death and sin,
- Sat down at the right hand of God the Father, and
- Sent the Holy Spirit to comfort and empower us every day

What kind of love is this? Who can refuse such a love?

Decision Time

The desperation of God to redeem mankind to Himself must be as evident as the nose on your face by now. That desperation led to the death of Jesus through unimaginable pain and suffering so that you might be saved from spiritual death.

Despite that demonstration of unspeakable love, some men still resist, thinking there must be another way. They think it is narrow minded and bigoted to think Jesus is the only way to God.

My friend, I am only the mouthpiece and messenger. I can only offer Jesus' own words,

> Jesus answered, "I am the *Way* and the *Truth* and the *Life*. No one comes to the Father except through *Me*."   John 14:6 NIV

The blood and death of Christ on that cross ... the empty tomb ... His resurrection and ascension ... and His own words clearly *confront, convict,* and *call* you to make a decision. Yes or No. Accept the Truth or forever deal with the consequences.

You can step through the *Cross*, accept Christ as Savior and make Him Lord of your life. Or you can reject the love of God and the offer of forgiveness/reconciliation through Christ.

The consequences of this second choice are this: You will continue to find yourself stuck in desperate places, taking "toll roads" that lead you further in, upon which you will never find your way out.

My fervent prayer is two-fold. First, if you are desperate and do not know Christ as your Savior, you will see that He is your only hope. Second, if you are a follower of Christ but wavering in your faith or walking apart from Him, remember what He has done for you. Return to Christ and His unconditional love, and allow Him to take you out of your desperate place.

Questions Every Desperate Man Needs to Answer

1) It sounds strange to write and talk about "the desperation of God." Why was God desperate and what did He do about it?

2) Three *meanings* of the Cross were cited. What were they and why do you think Jesus was willing to endure them?
   a) _____ Reason: _____

   b) _____ Reason: _____

   c) _____ Reason: _____

3) Four *messages* of the Cross were discussed that lead to a crisis of decision. List them below.
   a)
   b)
   c)
   d)

4) What is the "crisis of decision?"

5) Have you made the decision to receive Christ as your personal Savior? If not, why not?

Personal Reflections on My Journey:

PART THREE

The Journey Home: *A Call to Desperate Living*

Introduction

In this third and last part of our journey, we take an intentional right turn. From this point forward what I have to say is directed to men who know Christ is their Savior and want to understand what it means to make Him Lord of our lives and how to live desperately for Him.

That said, I want to leave this open invitation for all men to keep walking with us on this journey, even if you have not become a follower of Christ. My hope is the wonderful story of the transformation of the caterpillar into a butterfly that follows will be just the metaphor you need to better understand God's amazing creation and how He uses it to reveal Himself and draw us into a personal relationship with Him through Jesus.

Then I want to show you how that same kind of transformational process occurs in the lives of desperate Christian men and provide examples of what it means to *live desperately* for God the rest of the way Home by the power of His Holy Spirit.

Finally, we will revisit our five friends to see how their lives turned out. Did they wake up and smell the sweet fragrant aroma of the blood of Christ poured out for them on the cross? Or did they continue to make bad decisions that held them in desperate places or took them even deeper into despair?

I am so grateful you have read to this point and pray you will finish and be blessed for doing so. As I said before, God showed His desperation through the Cross of Christ because He loves us so much and wants to adopt us as sons. Once in the family, our faithful Father will never let go or lose sight of us even when we wander back into desperate places.

CHAPTER NINE

"Lord, Make Me a butterfly"

I confess I remembered little about butterflies from my high school biology other than the obvious—they come from caterpillars, can be very beautiful, and you don't see many flying around. So I took to the Internet to refresh my memory. I learned a few new things and quickly became overwhelmed with more than I needed to know.

The four stages in the life cycle of the butterfly represent one of the most amazing examples of God's handiwork in nature. I found it interesting that the total life cycle of butterflies through all four stages averages just six to eight weeks. That seemed shorter than I would have imagined, given all they go through to get to the last stage. Perhaps because each stage is so abbreviated, they are very focused and highly mission-minded.

Stage 1: Eggs. Female butterflies lay very tiny eggs with great care on the leaves of plants. It was interesting to learn they only lay their eggs on the types of plants the soon-to-emerge caterpillars will eat. The female butterfly spaces her eggs in positions and places that will provide enough food for each to survive and grow. The eggs hatch within a few days.

Stage 2: Caterpillars. The emergent tiny larva or caterpillars are born eaters, beginning with the leaves on which they are born. Since they remain in that stage for only a couple of weeks, they eat virtually non-stop to grow as quickly as possible and shed their skins (molt) several times during the process. When the growth period is over, the caterpillar finds a good place to "hang around" on the underside of a leaf or twig. Then perhaps the most amazing transformation process in nature begins—the metamorphosis of the caterpillar.

Stage 3: Chrysalis. The caterpillar begins its transformation process through the creation of a chrysalis, a hard protective shell that encases this amazing set of events. During this process, the caterpillar begins to melt away. It actually digests itself as its DNA is transformed into that which creates the butterfly. The process takes seven to ten days, producing one of the most beautiful and fragile of all creations emerges.

Stage 4: Butterfly. Despite all the effort and amazing metamorphosis required to produce a butterfly, the average life expectancy is typically only a couple of weeks. The butterfly exists for one purpose—to reproduce itself. The female butterfly mates once, lays eggs, and dies. Mission accomplished.

The Butterfly Analogy: God's Transformative Process in Man
The infinite wisdom of God spoke the world into existence.

> *"By faith we understand that the universe was formed at God's command, so that what is seen was not made out of what was visible."* Hebrews 11:3 NIV

From the dawn of creation, God knew that one day man would observe and understand the science of different life forms, e.g., human, animal, and insect. He also knew that, as Christians immersed themselves in the Bible studying the nature of God, we would see the magnificence of His creation in nature. Butterflies are among God's most beautiful and unique creations; they cause us to consider the similitude to His handiwork in the lives of people.

Perhaps that explains why butterflies exist and have such a unique life cycle. This side of Heaven we will not know, but we do know throughout His Word, God wove the stages of the life cycle of the butterfly for our benefit. Consider these transformational analogies.

The Egg: While we may not understand exactly the science behind it, butterfly DNA is "pre-programmed" to transform into a tiny larva that will become a full grown caterpillar. The larva grows within the secure space of the egg shell until it can no longer contain the growing caterpillar. Ultimately, the caterpillar emerges and gets to work.

God *pre-programmed* within our human DNA the knowledge of Himself and a "longing for eternity"—a relationship with Him. Solomon, considered the wisest and richest man who ever lived, used that knowledge and wisdom to experience as much in creation as he could. Consider his insightful observation:

> *"He has made everything beautiful in its time. He has also set eternity in the human heart; yet no one can fathom what God has done from beginning to end."* Ecclesiastes 3:11 NIV

Perhaps Solomon learned the deep truth of that statement from hanging around his dad, King David. David wrote numerous psalms with great passion for God. This verse demonstrates a heart that was hungry for the Lord:

> *"As the deer pants for streams of water, so my soul pants for you, O God. My soul thirsts for God, for the living God. When can I go and meet with God?"* Psalm 42:1-2 NIV

The brilliant French mathematician, physicist, inventor, and Christian philosopher, Blaise Pascal, made the following famous quote,

> *"There is a God-shaped vacuum in the heart of every man which cannot be filled by any created thing, but only by God the Creator, made known through Jesus Christ."*

Desperate men who long to do things their own way reject these teachings. They replace the God-given DNA that brings an internal longing for God with every conceivable external pleasure that satisfies their flesh and appeases their minds.

We know such things cannot satiate their spiritual thirsts. Only God can do that. King Solomon also provided bad examples as well as good ones. He was drawn away from God by marrying many foreign wives who worshiped other gods. To appease them, Solomon became tolerant (a popular word among unbelievers today) of their gods and lost the zeal and passion for the Lord God alone.

In the book of Ecclesiastes (written by Solomon), we read of the frustration and discouragement he experienced because his massive wealth and wisdom did not satisfy him. He bought the lies of Satan through the voices of many outside influences that seemed *tolerant* to him at the time. They nearly destroyed him, and he lost the joy of the Lord he once knew when he walked closely with God in the righteous ways of his father, David. Solomon's tolerance and distraction eventually led to the destruction of his kingdom.

So my desperate brothers, let this be a reminder that our longing and thirsting for God can only be satisfied through an intimate relationship with Him and not the world. Allow the longing in your heart for God to burst forth for His good will and pleasure, that for which it was designed. Then, and then only, will you find the joy of the Lord that fills our hearts and peace of mind.

The Caterpillar. Born to die—what a purpose in life! What can we learn from the short life of the caterpillar when apparently all it does is eat itself to death? Let me suggest three takeaways.

First, the caterpillar eats only that which helps it grow and complete its intended purpose. Two verses come to mind that apply to men and what we "eat."

> "*Your words (the Scriptures) and I **ate** them and Your words became for me a joy and the delight of my heart for I have been called by Your name O Lord God of Hosts.*" Jeremiah 15:16 NASB

> "*Like newborn babies, crave pure spiritual milk, so that by it you may grow up in your salvation*" 1 Peter 2:2 NIV

The Word of God provides "spiritual food" without which we will either die (in the spiritual sense) or grow into something other than that which God intended because we gorged ourselves on every food the world provided. Solomon provided a good example of both.

Second, caterpillars consume all they can while they can. They stay focused on the task at hand until a genetic switch tells them to stop. As Christian men, we need to do the same—continue to read and digest the Word daily until He comes for us or calls us home.

Finally, the caterpillar surrenders to a greater purpose. This may seem a bit overly dramatic, but in the insect world perhaps not so much. If the caterpillar is going to become a butterfly, it has to give itself up to that end. In the same way, Jesus came to die. His purpose could only be fulfilled in His death. For by His death, we have life.

> "*For even the Son of Man did not come to be served, but to serve, and to give his life as a ransom for many.*" Mark 10:45 NASB

The Chrysalis. The metamorphosis that takes place within the chrysalis changes the very nature of one of God's creations into another. We can say the caterpillar dies to itself and becomes a new creation.

In the same way, the Cross of Christ, His death, and resurrection provided the means for that kind of transformation in men. Consider how well this process is represented in Scripture.

> *"Therefore, if anyone is in Christ, the new creation has come: The old has gone, the new is here!"* 2 Corinthians 5:17 NIV

But it does not stop there. The metamorphosis continues. ***It begins in the mind*** by changing the way we think because that really controls our lives, what we do, how we act, etc. The Apostle Paul wrote,

> *"And do not be conformed to this world, but be transformed by the renewing of your mind, so that you may prove what the will of God is, that which is good and acceptable and perfect."* Romans 12:2 NASB

The transformation continues *in the heart of man*. This verse represents this process very well:

> *"Rend your hearts and not your garments…"* Joel 2:13 NIV

Rending garments refers to the practice in which Jews tore their outer garments when struck by grief or some other outrage, including things they considered blasphemies or sin. Like many such practices, it became a ritual rather than a true expression of the heart for repentance. Therefore, through the prophet, Joel, God calls them out. He wants men with truly repentant hearts not just those practicing religious acts, tearing their clothes.

In his most penitent psalm, King David demonstrated his understanding of what God wanted. David had been caught in his sins of adultery and murder. Nathan, the prophet of God to whom David listened, called him out. In Psalm 51, the broken and humiliated king wrote,

> *"For You do not delight in sacrifice, otherwise I would give it … The sacrifices of God are a broken spirit; a broken and a contrite heart, O God, You will not despise."* Psalm 51:16-17 NASB

Finally, there is one more part of the transformation process we need to consider—agendas. The caterpillar has one agenda, while the butterfly has a completely different one. Somewhere in the DNA conversion that manifests the physical transformation, *the motives of the new creation are changed.*

That should hold true for transformed Christian men as well. Our motives and agendas should be in process of transformation into those that delight the heart of God. Consider the words of James.

> *"You ask and do not receive, because you ask with wrong motives, so that you may spend it on your pleasures."*   James 4:3 NASB

In the Sermon on the Mount, Jesus told His disciples and thousands who listened that they should be "pure in heart." He further subrogated any other agenda people wanted or expected of Him. He completely sold out to God. In His greatest moment of stress, He prayed,

> *"Father, if You are willing, take this cup from Me; yet not My will, but Yours be done."*   Luke 22:42 NIV

That should be our prayer. I learned over many years, for most of us, it takes a while to get there.

The Butterfly. As stated previously, butterflies exist for one purpose: *to reproduce themselves.* Jesus made that command clear to His disciples that remains or marching orders today.

> *"…All authority has been given to Me in heaven and on earth. Go therefore and make disciples of all the nations, baptizing them in the name of the Father and the Son and the Holy Spirit, teaching them to observe all that I commanded you; and lo, I am with you always, even to the end of the age."*
>   Matthew 28: 18-20 NASB

Butterflies are very delicate and nearly defenseless against their predators: birds, spiders, reptiles, and other insects. Their best defense is camouflage. They try to blend in with their surroundings so they cannot be seen.

Sadly, this describes too many "camouflage Christians." They do not want to stick out or be noticed. That mindset is the root cause of many problems today in our nation and the world in which we live. We are supposed to *stand out*.

Jesus' Great Commission to all of His disciples begins with the only words we need to hear. *"All power has been given to me in heaven and on earth."* Being an effective witness or warrior does not depend on our power (fortunately). The power of God *transforms* us through the Holy Spirit. Then He *transfers* all the power we need to accomplish this mandate.

Energized and equipped by that transforming power, the *going, baptizing,* and *teaching* become possible. To encourage His disciples further, Jesus offered those words to which all desperate Christians cling today. "I've got your back." (My paraphrase.) Jesus really said, "I am with you always." Our omnipresent God never leaves us alone…no matter what or where!

I close this chapter with the same words I chose for the title – a short, powerful prayer of a man desperate for more of God:

"Lord, make me a butterfly."

Questions Every Desperate Man Needs to Answer

We see the handiwork of God in the transformation process of a caterpillar into a butterfly. However, too often we see new and old Christians who have stunted or stopped the process. Consider these three observations.

- Stuck in your cocoon — afraid to let God finish His work in you.
- Living the "camouflage life" that keeps you from standing out as a Christian.
- Huddling up with like-minded butterflies, long on staying but short on going as Jesus commanded.

1) How do men get stuck in their cocoons?

2) Why do men prefer to hide or camouflage their faith?

3) What are some ways to break up the "holy huddles" and move men out of our comfort zones into places of ministry like Jesus commanded?

Personal Reflections on My Journey:

Write down your thoughts on any of those three areas that apply to your life.

_____
_____
_____
_____
_____

CHAPTER TEN

What We Learn from Butterflies Can Change the World

The last chapter focused our attention on the development and life cycle of caterpillars and butterflies in order to draw useful analogies to our lives as developing Christian men – our transformation process. In this chapter, we turn our attention to lessons we can learn from the short life of the butterfly that demonstrate our ongoing transformational process and have the potential for having a Christ-like impact on our world.

Lesson #1: Dying to self. Just as the caterpillar is born to die, so too are Christians. When we are born again (John 3), we should begin immediately to learn what it means to die to self. But I'm not referring to physical death. Rather, it is the form of death about which Jesus spoke most often as He taught His disciples what it meant to *live desperately.*

> "And He was saying to them all, "If anyone wishes to come after Me, he must **deny himself**, and **take up his cross daily** and follow Me."
> Luke 9:23 NASB

Jesus' teachings on this difficult subject are not so much difficult to understand as they are difficult to live out. The Apostle Paul echoed and exemplified Jesus' words when he wrote:

> "I have been **crucified with Christ**. It is no longer I who live, but Christ who lives in me."   Galatians 2:20 NASB

> "I affirm, brethren, by the boasting in you which I have in Christ Jesus our Lord, **I die daily**."   1 Corinthians 15:31 NASB

"Denying oneself." "Taking up your cross daily." "Dying daily."

When Jesus used such language even His disciples pulled back. They knew exactly what He meant. As we noted previously, a cross in Roman times meant one thing—death. Jesus went to great lengths to help His disciples wrap their arms around this essential lesson for being a real, committed Christ follower; not a spectator, but an authentic participant completely sold out to Christ. This is hard stuff, not for the faint of heart or desperate men only partially committed.

If those verses do not establish the importance and critical nature of this principle, *dying to self,* you need to pause and reconsider your position and motives. Dying to self begins the greatest transformation in life after salvation.

We become desperate for more of Him than more from Him.

Lesson #2: Avoid "butterfly burnout." As I noted previously, butterflies burn out and die in as little as two weeks. Human power runs down like a battery—it starts strong and slowly fades to the point it will not allow one more mouse click.

Christian men, desperate for more of God, quickly learn how easy it is to burn out or experience a personal power outage when we operate in our own strength. God did not intend for us to work in that way. He knew the limitations of men because He created us with them. Why would He do that? To ensure we learn to depend on Him "for all things, in all things, and through all things."

Jesus provided the source of this power. The Holy Spirit. During the Last Supper, Jesus shared a number of things that greatly troubled His disciples. Twice He said He was *going away* so the Holy Spirit could *come*. Curious words. Following is an excerpt of that teaching.

> *"But I tell you the truth, it is to your advantage that I go away; for if I do not go away, the Helper [Holy Spirit] will not come to you; but if I go, I will send Him to you."* John 16: 7 NASB

Those words were spoken *before* the Crucifixion. I doubt the disciples understood what Jesus was saying. They were still trying to grasp the part about His death.

After His resurrection, Jesus reminded them of the promise He would send the Holy Spirit to be their guide, comforter, and **source of power** so they would not have to live by their own strength.

Just before Jesus ascended into Heaven, He spoke these last words to His disciples:

> *"But you will receive **power** when the Holy Spirit comes upon you; you shall be My witnesses both in Jerusalem, and in all Judea and Samaria, even to the remotest part of the earth."* Acts 1:8 NASB

Power for what? Power to *go*. Power to *make disciples*. Power to *be His witnesses*, despite all kinds of opposition and demonic attacks. Power that is available to us today and must be accessed for us to live desperately for Christ as He defined it. The Holy Spirit alone provides this power. The journey Home is a marathon not a sprint, and it takes sustained power to finish the race.

Lesson #3: Every day matters. Butterflies make the best of their short lives. Many men live like we think we will live forever. I am not suggesting we live in sprint mode in contradiction of my closing comment above. I am stating emphatically that every day matters and that should dictate, in large part, how we live. James, the half-brother of Jesus and leader of the new Christian church, shared his wisdom regarding this important lesson.

> *"Now listen, you who say, 'Today or tomorrow we will go to this or that city, spend a year there, carry on business and make money.' Why, you do not even know what will happen tomorrow. What is your life? You are a mist that appears for a little while and then vanishes. Instead you ought to say, 'If it is the Lord's will, we will live and do this or that.' As it is, you boast in your arrogant schemes. All such boasting is evil."*
>
> James 4:13-16 NIV

Three takeaways from this short passage of Scripture reinforce this lesson that every day matters:

- *Life is a vapor.* That means life this side of Home is very short. You have precious little time to make an impact.
- *Taking tomorrow for granted.* Making assumptions about tomorrow is foolish. James called it boastful, arrogant. God gives us what we need for today just like manna. You may recall manna was only good for the day it fell from Heaven.
- *Live each day in accordance with the will of God and leave the results to Him.* Finding the will of God is not nearly as hard to discern as we think it is. The key is to seek Him and ask!

Every day matters to God. Every day is a gift from our loving heavenly Father. Whether you are on vacation, playing golf, taking in His amazing creation, worshipping, witnessing, or working, God wants you to enjoy what He has given to you ... *this day.* The abundant Christian life, to which Jesus referred, was meant to be lived to the fullest and all of that to the glory of God in all things.

Lesson #4: Replicating the love and life of Christ everywhere you land. As I said previously, butterflies exist for one reason. To lay eggs—replicate themselves. Then they die. But while they live, they fly from leaf to leaf laying eggs that will yield more larvae, caterpillars, and butterflies. That cycle will go on until the Lord says stop.

Jesus gave His disciples that same homework assignment: *multiplication*. Jesus prepared, empowered, and sent His disciples to minister to others in ways we can replicate. Here are four keys to successfully replicating ourselves He taught and modeled for His disciples.

1) Jesus told them the key to success: "Love one another." (John 15: 12 NASB)

2) The two ways to approach people. Jesus used only two adjectives to describe Himself. "I am gentle and humble in heart." (Matthew 11:29 NASB)

3) Lead by example in serving others. *"After that, he poured water into a basin and began to wash his disciples' feet,"* (John 13: 5a NIV)

4) He sent them out. "…go and make disciples." (Matthew 28: 19 NIV)

I thought you would be interested in the results of Jesus' three-year ministry that began with a small group of disciples. Over 2.2 billion people in the world today say they are Christians!

Questions Every Desperate Man Needs to Answer

List the four lessons we can learn from the different stages of the life cycle of a butterfly and its transformation process.

1.
2.
3.
4.

1) What does "dying to self" look like to you?

2) "Butterfly burnout" means operating on one's own power instead that available from the Holy Spirit. Why do men choose the former over the latter? What does operating in the power of the Holy Spirit look like?

3) "Every day matters" implies living like this is your last day on earth. If you really believed that was the case, what would you do differently? What prevents you from living like that?

4) What does "replicating the love and life of Christ" look like in practical applications?

Personal Reflections on My Journey:

CHAPTER ELEVEN

Evidence of Desperate Living

Recall when you and I were on trial for our lives before we knew Christ as Savior, we were unable to present *evidence* that proved we deserved to be found innocent. We learned and experienced firsthand that Christ alone is able to save and redeem condemned men. Hallelujah for that!

Now that we are in Christ, we never have to stand trial again. But that does not mean we do not have to provide evidence that demonstrates to the world we are indeed born again and being transformed, like the caterpillar, into a beautiful representation of Jesus – His life and legacy.

Following are five expressions of our gratitude to God for His amazing Gift of salvation, Jesus. We want to be "caught in the act" for any and all of them as often as we can. Remember they are expressions of our love and appreciation back to God and not done because we feel like we have to or under compulsion which would be wrong reasons and spoil the gift.

Loving
When asked, "What is the greatest commandment of all?" Jesus replied,

> *"Jesus answered, the foremost is, 'HEAR, O ISRAEL! THE LORD OUR GOD IS ONE LORD; AND YOU SHALL LOVE THE LORD YOUR GOD WITH ALL YOUR HEART, AND WITH ALL YOUR SOUL, AND WITH ALL YOUR MIND, AND WITH ALL YOUR STRENGTH.' THE SECOND IS THIS, 'YOU SHALL LOVE YOUR NEIGHBOR AS YOURSELF.' THERE IS NO OTHER COMMANDMENT GREATER THAN THESE."* Mark 12:29-31 NASB

Jesus lived the perfect example of loving desperately; the ultimate example was laying down His life for you and me. The Apostle Paul wrote the best description in the most famous words on the subject of Jesus' kind of love.

> *"Love is patient, love is kind and is not jealous; love does not brag and is not arrogant, does not act unbecomingly; it does not seek its own, is not provoked, does not take into account a wrong suffered, does not rejoice in unrighteousness, but rejoices with the truth; bears all things, believes all things, hopes all things, endures all things. Love never fails."* 1 Corinthians 13: 4-8a NASB

Desperate living means we strive to love others no matter how desperate or despised they may be in the eyes of the world. Never forget that when we remained in our sin, we were just as pitiful as anyone else. God loved us then as He does now. Loving others is evidence of our obedience to Jesus' command "that you love one another, even as I have loved you..." John 13:34 NASB

Praying-Praising

I joined the two together because both present strong evidence of a renewed heart now desperate for more of God. Regarding prayer, who do you consider the greatest prayer warrior in the Bible? Abraham? Moses? David? The Apostle Paul? Let me suggest another name: Jesus.

Multiple times in the Gospels we read that Jesus made it a priority to "get alone to pray." He set the example for all of us when it comes to the content and frequency of prayer.

> *"In the early morning, while it was still dark, Jesus got up, left the house, and went away to a secluded place, and was praying there."* Mark 1:35 NASB

The Apostle Paul's words incorporate both evidences – *praising* and *praying* with a heart of *thanksgiving*.

> *"Rejoice always; pray without ceasing; in everything give thanks; for this is God's will for you in Christ Jesus."* 1 Thessalonians 5: 16-18 NASB

Praying without ceasing is not a command to do nothing but pray all day. Rather it asserts that Christians should maintain a prayerful mindset throughout the day to stay connected to the source. Desperate living is enabled and empowered by prayer.

Praise is actually a subset of prayer. No one in Scripture wrote more about praising God than David, the humble shepherd who became king. His praise was alive with singing, dancing, and worshiping before the Lord. Here are a few examples to help us understand what this looks like.

> *"The heavens declare the glory of God, the skies proclaims His hands."* Psalm 19:1 NIV

> *"But Thou art holy, O Thou that inhabits the praises of Israel."* Psalm 22:3 KJV

> *"I will extol thee, my God, O king; and I will bless thy name forever and ever. Every day will I bless thee; and I will praise thy name forever and ever. Great is the LORD, and greatly to be praised; and his greatness is unsearchable. One generation shall praise thy works to another, and shall declare thy mighty acts."* Psalm 145: 1-4 KJV

The last set of verses are some of my favorites I memorized years ago to use when I just wanted to praise God and did not have my Bible around to look them up. I do not know what your praise looks like in private or public. Very often great saints of old used their praise as the entry point into times of prayer, which leads to the next place God loves to catch men.

Believing

Jesus said that *unbelief* kept Him from doing miracles in His hometown. Where there was no faith or belief, nothing could happen. That is a strong indictment. As we consider this consequence of unbelief, let's begin with the man whose reputation for doubt and unbelief is well-known – Thomas.

After the crucifixion of Jesus, Thomas missed a meeting of the disciples during which Jesus made an appearance to provide evidence of His resurrection. Told what happened in his absence, Thomas made the famous reply that birthed the phrase "seeing is believing":

> *"Unless I see in His hands the imprint of the nails, and put my finger into the place of the nails, and put my hand into His side, I will not believe."*
> John 20:25 NASB

Thomas followed Jesus for three years, yet he still did not believe what Jesus consistently said to the disciples. He would be put to death and then rise from the dead after three days.

Much to Thomas' delight and shame, Jesus appeared to the disciples again when he was present. Jesus went straight to Thomas and instructed him do those things He said would make him believe, i.e., put his fingers in Jesus' side and see the holes in His hands. After Thomas confessed his belief that Jesus was indeed God, he received a gentle rebuke from Jesus, one that fits many of us today.

> *"…do not be unbelieving, but believing."*   John 20:27 NASB

Faith is not faith if you can know the result beforehand. If we were honest, each of us would admit to times in our lives when we could substitute our names in place of Thomas'. The writer of Hebrews added another layer to the importance of *believing*:

> *"...without faith it is **impossible** to please God..."*   Hebrews 11:6 NIV

Emphasis on the word *impossible*. The hard truth is this: Faith, or the lack thereof, separates believers from unbelievers. And as we have seen (and experienced), it also separates "unbelieving believers" from strong men of faith pressing on toward desperate living. The writer of Hebrews also wrote, *"Faith is the **evidence** of things unseen."*

Giving

Search the Gospels and you will find Jesus spoke more about a man and his money than Heaven and Hell combined. Jesus knew we learn much about the heart of a man from his attitude and actions in the area of giving. It provided physical ***evidence*** of our gratitude.

Giving is an act of worship. Many people, including some Christians, view giving as a ritual churches practice each week. That way of thinking is way off base. For New Testament Christians, it began here:

> *"For God so loved the world, that He **gave** His only begotten Son..."*
>   John 3:16 NASB

We give back to God in response to His generous expression of that love, the gift of salvation in Christ. God's Gift prompts ours. This simple truth makes clear the first and purest motive.

There is another reason that is a bit startling because of His directness:

> *"Will a man rob God? Yet you are robbing Me! But you say, 'How have we robbed You?' In tithes and offerings."*   Micah 3:8 NASB

This ought to get our attention. God called His own people thieves! God demands we give back to Him. God would not stand by and let His greedy, selfish people get away with using the money or wealth He had given them on things that dishonored Him.

Then there is our attitude toward giving. The Apostle Paul addressed that with young Christians in Corinth.

> *"Every man according as he purposes in his heart, so let him give; not grudgingly, or of necessity: for God loves a cheerful giver."*   2 Corinthians 9:7 KJV

God loves it when His people give in this manner. One of the greatest changes in my life came as a young man when the Holy Spirit made the following change in my heart toward giving. He showed me that giving to God (and others in need) is something I "get to do," not "have to do."

One more story on giving. The story of the "Widow's Mite" is one of the first Bible lessons taught to any child in Sunday school. Read it again and process Jesus' response.

> *"(Jesus) sat down opposite the treasury and began observing how the people were putting money into the treasury. Many rich people were putting in large sums. A poor widow came and put in two small copper coins, which amount to a cent. Calling His disciples to Him, He said to them, 'Truly I say to you, this poor widow put in more than all the contributors to the treasury; for they all gave out of their surplus, but she gave out of her poverty, putting in all she owned, all she had to live on.'"*   Mark 12: 41-44 NASB

Most of us who give faithfully do so out of surplus – what is left over. We cannot really conceive of doing what this poor widow did. How could she give it all away? How would she live, eat, pay her bills? The answer is simple. Simple faith. She lived by faith and the belief that Jehovah Jireh (God our Provider) would meet her needs as He always had. That is all the evidence we need.

Serving

To serve others, we do not have to be rich, particularly smart, or even well-trained. It does not always require traveling great distances around the world to find places to engage. The most important ability required is *availability*.

One positive trend in our country in recent years, particularly among young people, is greater involvement in volunteering and helping others. "Pay it forward" became a popular phrase. Many companies created "service days" in which people take a day off work to do something good for people in their community. People engaged in such acts of kindness and serving others set great examples for all, including Christians. But Christians ought to be the ones leading and setting the best and most examples.

On more than one occasion, the Apostle Paul admonished and encouraged Christians to examine our hearts when it came to how we live and the examples we set for others, especially those who are not believers. Jesus provided the best examples of serving we need.

> *"just as the Son of Man did not come to be served, but to serve, and to give His life as a ransom for many."*   Matthew 20:28 NASB

No greater example of humility in attitude and action exists. Jesus walked this earth with a singular focus on why He came—to *save sinners*. During His journey to the cross, we find Him *serving* people from all walks of life with every need imaginable expecting nothing in return.

One of the best known of all Bible stories is the Good Samaritan in Luke 10:25-37. Jesus tells of a Jewish traveler who had been beaten and robbed. Two religious men walked past the wounded man and did nothing to help. Then a third man stopped and cared for him. The caregiver came from different ethnic and religious backgrounds that Jews hated—he was a Samaritan.

Jesus asked His listeners, *"Which of these three was the good neighbor to the man who fell into the hands of the robbers?"* One replied, *"The one who showed him mercy."*

The Good Samaritan's acts of compassion and service provide compelling evidence we must imitate. Jesus ended the story with what He expects of all desperate men who follow Him:

"Go and do likewise."

Questions Every Desperate Man Needs to Answer

We discussed five behaviors that provide evidence of men living desperately. List them below.

1. _____ ☐ Insufficient Evidence ☐ Guilty
2. _____ ☐ Insufficient Evidence ☐ Guilty
3. _____ ☐ Insufficient Evidence ☐ Guilty
4. _____ ☐ Insufficient Evidence ☐ Guilty
5. _____ ☐ Insufficient Evidence ☐ Guilty

1) If you were on trial for impersonating a Christian, what verdict would be entered for each of the five behaviors shown above? Which ones need the most work? What are you doing to move the needle toward "guilty"?

2) What are some other examples of evidences of men living desperately?

Personal Reflections on My Journey:

CHAPTER TWELVE

Five Desperate Men (Reprised)

Throughout our lives, God puts people in our paths and allows untoward circumstances for one purpose: *Get our attention.* He wants our attention first, then our lives. Throughout history, men ignored His warnings. Many simply chose to disobey and went their own ways.

We left each of our five friends in a desperate place with life-altering choices to make. For these men there really were just two choices: God's way that led to the foot of the Cross of Christ or the toll road of their making that would lead them in deeper. Which path did they choose?

The Addict: *A Journey to Hope*
Now homeless, hungry, and hooked, James had nowhere to turn. The only good news from the bottom of life is the only way is up unless you choose to stay down. On occasion, James took a meal at a local rescue mission. He was annoyed that to get fed, they required him to sit in a Christian service and listen to someone talk about the gospel.

One night as "fate" would have it, during one of these services the preacher said something that pierced James' heart. The sermon covered Titus 3, but James heard only a few of the words. It was as if the speaker shouted those words and whispered the rest.

*"For we also one were foolish ourselves, disobedient, deceived, **enslaved to various lusts and pleasures,** spending our life in malice and envy, hateful, hating one another. But when the **kindness of God** our Savior and His love for mankind appeared, **He saved us,** not on the basis of deeds which we have done in righteousness, but **according to His mercy,** by the washing of regeneration and renewing by the Holy Spirit whom He poured out upon us richly through Jesus Christ our Savior, so that being justified by His grace we would be made heirs according to the hope of eternal life."*   Titus 3:3-7 NASB

James was overwhelmed with grief and "the godly sorrow that produces repentance." He surrendered his heart and life to Christ that night. After speaking with counselors there, he entered one of the rescue mission's life-recovery programs. It would not be easy. Every day would be a struggle to overcome the need and temptation and stop listening to the lies of Satan that had filled his ears for so many years.

Now James had a new power to live and a peace he had never known. For the first time in his life, he was in a good place where he wanted to stay. And for the first time James had hope for a future apart from addiction. He found being a desperate man on this side of the Cross was not only something he could live with … it was something he could not live without!

The Prisoner: *A Journey to Freedom*
Anger and resentment built up over a lifetime create prisons without bars for those who cannot forgive. Joe Jr. lived in such a prison. He hated his dad and wanted nothing to do with him.

Rather than join his father in the prison ministry group, JJ joined a prison gang out of spite. But Joe Sr. did not give up on his son or God. He continued to pray daily for JJ's deliverance and salvation. But would it ever come? Only God could tear down the prison walls within the heart of his son, built in anger, reinforced with hate.

Gang life in a prison is not much different than on the outside. Rivalries exist that often lead to fights and men getting hurt, some severely. JJ fell victim to such a war between rival gangs and ended up in the prison hospital. His injuries were severe to life-threatening.

In and out of consciousness, he had a dream in which the events of his life passed before him. He began to feel very cold and had a sense he was fading away. He wondered if this was what dying felt like. For the first time in his life, he admitted to himself he was desperate and afraid to die.

As JJ lay there waiting to die, he heard his dad's voice. He could not see him, but he heard him clearly. Joe Sr. was pleading with his son for forgiveness. He confessed to making many mistakes and not being there for him. Then he spoke words JJ had never heard from any man in his life: "I love you, son. I know you hate me for not being there for you. I am not asking you to love me, but I am asking you to forgive me. I learned here that God loves me and forgave my sins because of Jesus. He forgave me, I hope you can."

When Joe Jr. regained consciousness, for the first time since coming to prison, he asked to see his dad. Arrangements were made and Joe Sr. soon showed up at the door of his room. Joe Sr. timidly walked over to the bedside of his son. Joe Jr. slowly extended his arms toward his dad. For the first time, the two men embraced. They wept together for a long time.

Joe Jr. whispered in his dad's ear. "I forgive you, dad. I love you." He went on to tell his dad about the dream and hearing his voice. Then he shared the most amazing part. He told his dad that, before he regained consciousness, he asked Jesus to come into his life to save and set him free. Joe Sr. fell to his knees, weeping loudly, and gave a shout to the Lord. For the first time in his life, Joe Jr. was free.

"So if the Son makes you free, you will be free indeed."   John 8:36 NASB

The Rich Man: *A Journey to Humility*
We left our wealthy friend, Charles, in a desperate place. He was consumed by the need to restore the family fortune that evaporated during the market downturn and led to his father's suicide. He became a second generation workaholic, following in his father's footsteps.

Work occupied his days and violated his nights, keeping him away from his family. Ignoring his wife's pleading for him to relent and spend time with them, he pressed on, certain that rebuilding his fortune would save his marriage and family. After all, he thought, losing it is what doomed his family when he was a boy.

Then one night, Charles came home very late to a dark house. Upon entering, he found it empty. Stunned by the solitude, he called out to his wife and kids, but there was no answer. He groped around in the dark looking for a light switch, and after turning on a lamp on the Chippendale table, he found a note. It was from his wife, letting him know they had moved out. She did not say where they went. One final dagger: the note also said she had filed for divorce on the grounds of abandonment.

Needless to say, Charles was shocked. Desperate to find his family, he called his wife's cell phone. No answer. He called her parents' home. Same result. Feeling more alone that he ever had, Charles went into his study and sat down to a bottle of Scotch. His mind began to play tricks on him as he thought about his father's decision to commit suicide.

Charles reached in the drawer of what used to be his father's desk. He pulled out the pistol his father had used to commit that grievous act and wondered if his life should end in the same way. He leaned forward with his head in his hands, placing his elbows on the desk.

Looking down, his eyes glanced at a picture his daughter had drawn and given him some years before; one he had essentially ignored. But this time the picture and her words caught his attention. It was a picture of an empty cross with the following words underneath. "Jesus loves you, daddy, and so do I."

And with that, proud and aloof Charles finally broke. Tears poured down his face into the glass of Scotch. He slowly put the gun back in the drawer and poured the remaining drink down the drain of the wet bar. After his father's death, Charles had quit praying and believing in God. But now he knelt beside his father's desk and prayed for the first time since he was a boy.

Clutching his daughter's picture in his hand, Charles cried out to God to save him from the gods of wealth and work. He asked for salvation in his own life and reconciliation for his family. God answered the first request immediately. The second answer came over time.

Years of being alone and overlooked at first produced a few scars in the mind of Charles' wife. Over time, they began to callous over. Charles would have to work hard to prove his love and devotion, first to his wife, then his family.

Reconciliation. Charles went from reconciling the balance sheets of a committed workaholic to accepting God's form of reconciliation in Christ. Then came the hard part—reconciling his relationship with his wife and family.

> *"For what does it profit a man to gain the whole world and forfeit his soul?"*
> Mark 8: 36 NASB

The Pastor: *A Journey to Healing*

Confronted with his not-so-secret sins, Pastor Thomas maintained he did not have an issue with pornography. This was just an isolated occurrence and would not happen again. But his computer URL histories suggested otherwise. Thomas was asked to resign his pulpit immediately or be fired. Throughout this embarrassing process, his wife stood beside him.

Defiant, Thomas began to look for another opportunity as a pastor hoping he could hide his secret sin from churches to which he applied. Interview after interview seemed to go well, but in the end, his past failure always seemed to find him out.

Financially in a desperate place, Thomas took a job at a large chain superstore, oddly enough in the computer department. Not every computer in the department had strong Internet filters, thus allowing Thomas to periodically feed his lust. This time somehow he managed not to get caught.

Thomas did his best to avoid former church members who shopped at the store. The humiliation was too great, and he continued to blame them for his abrupt change in circumstances. Where was the grace and forgiveness he had taught them so often in his sermons?

Thomas' home life began to deteriorate. Despite the faithfulness of his wife, their marriage was a shell of what it once was and his relationships with his kids were strained at best. Then the Holy Spirit intervened in a most amazing way. (What other way does He intervene?)

One day Thomas was sitting with his young son, trying desperately to reconnect with him. Out of nowhere, the boy looked him in the eye and asked for the first time, "Daddy, why aren't you a preacher anymore? Don't you love God anymore?" Thomas swallowed hard trying to think of an appropriate response. Before he could find one, his son dropped his head and said, "My friend said it is because you did something bad so God won't let you preach at His church anymore. Daddy, is that right?"

Confronted in a way he never imagined, by his own son, Thomas had finally arrived at his fork in the road. He could either lie to his son to keep his secret sin secret, or he could finally face his demons and tell the truth. As he pondered which path to choose, the Holy Spirit brought to mind this verse:

> *"Whoever conceals their sins does not prosper, but the one who confesses and renounces them finds mercy."*   Proverbs 28:13 NIV

Thomas wanted mercy. He called his wife into the room and, through his tears, began to openly confess his sin and beg her forgiveness. He went before the church and did the same thing. Now grace and forgiveness were found in abundance. Thomas could begin his healing process.

Upon completion of a long and strenuous counseling and restoration program, God called Thomas back into ministry—not to the pulpit, but to a counseling ministry to other pastors dealing with secret sins and their fallout. For the first time in his walk with the Lord, Thomas was finally at a place at which he was desperate for more *of* God than *from* God.

The Businessman (aka The Adulterer): *A Journey to Reconciliation*
The prognosis is not good. Psychologists estimate that only 30 percent of marriages in which there has been an extramarital affair survive. David decided he needed to come clean and confess his infidelity. Fear gripped him as he thought about how his wife will respond. Would she simply and silently take the kids and walk out? Would she yell and scream and call him names? He preferred the latter. But right now he was more concerned with mustering the courage to tell her, hoping she will forgive him (at some point in the future).

David's wife had sensed something was troubling him ever since he returned from his last business trip. But she was not about to press him; things between them had been strained enough in recent months. Finally one evening, after putting the kids to bed, David sat down with his wife and told her the whole sordid *affair*. No yelling or screaming. She did not walk out. She just cried, long and hard … very hard. David saw that her spirit was heart was broken and her spirit deeply wounded.

Unless a man has become hardened and indifferent, there is something about watching his wife sob uncontrollably, knowing he is the cause, that melts his heart like wax. Overwhelmed with guilt and remorse over his foolish acts of *lust fulfilled,* David broke down. He knelt beside his wife and wept harder than he ever had in his entire life.

For the first time in months, David took his wife into his arms and held her while they both wept. As the sobbing began to subside, David began to apologize and ask forgiveness. He was the one who suggested counseling and, for the first time in their marriage, thought it would be a good idea to find a good church to begin attending. A friend invited David and his family to attend church with him. It was a Bible-believing and teaching fellowship that had great programs for kids and, yes, they even let sinners like David attend.

David and his wife began the long climb back to restoration and reconciliation in their marriage. As I wrote earlier, the road into desperate places is often smooth and downhill; the road out bumpy and uphill. It took a lot of work and perseverance for them to successfully climb out. But they did it.

Questions Every Desperate Man Needs to Answer

We began and ended this journey looking into the lives of five men whose decisions led them into desperate places — decisions all men make at various points in our lives. As we wrap this up, I thought it would be a good exercise to begin by writing down lessons learned from their lives that have direct, or possibly indirect, application in ours. In the space provided, please write down one lesson you learned from the story of each of these five men.

1. James the Addict.

2. Joe Jr. the Prisoner.

3. Charles the Wealth Worshipper.

4. Pastor Thomas hiding Secret Sins.

5. David the Adulterer.

Epitaph Exercise: In the space provided, please write the words you would like to have put on your tombstone (assume you will have one). For example, I would write: "He lived desperately for God every day of his life."

Now write a summary of the words you would like to have shared at your memorial service.

To help you take what you learned from this book and move from *inspiration* to **application**, let's conclude with what I refer to as your "mini-plan" for desperate living. The goal is to help you live in accordance with your own words above in tandem with the Word of God and His plan for your life. His is a great plan—better than any we could contrive.

You may have seen or participated in something similar to the following at work or church. It is not rocket science, but this exercise can be a very effective tool IF you add the fourth element—accountability. Without that, these plans never last very long and sometimes never get out of the gate.

_____ **- My Mini-Plan for Desperate Living**

Stop. List three things you need to stop doing that may be leading you into desperate places, keeping you there, or hindering God from leading you out.

1. _____
   _____
   _____

2. _____
   _____
   _____

3. _____
   _____
   _____

Start. List three things you need to begin immediately to jumpstart or renew your growth and transformation into a man desperate for more of God and to live desperately for Him.

1. _____
   _____
   _____

2. _____
   _____
   _____

3. _____
   _____
   _____

Continue. List three things you are doing that lay down evidence in your life that would get you convicted of replicating the love and life of Christ everywhere you land.

1. _____
   _____

2. _____
   _____

3. _____
   _____

Accountability Decree: I hereby agree that I am willing to be held accountable for the words I have written for my epitaph and memorial service and the steps listed in this plan for the purpose of living desperately for Christ all the remaining days of my life.

_____
Your Signature Here

EPILOGUE

When I sat down to write this book, I felt the Holy Spirit gave me a clear outline in three parts. And it was to be written as a journey through your life.

The first part made the case that all men are desperate whether we admit it or not. And while I still cannot define a desperate man, I hope I was able to show you what we look like such that you identified with one or more of our five friends in some ways. I know I certainly do.

The second part was the pivot point. I wanted to emphasize the importance of establishing a relationship with Christ if you do not know Him and reassessing that relationship if you say you do. All roads really do lead to the cross; it is there our lives pivot in that we are reborn in Christ or we choose to remain in desperate places. Why would any man do that? Life is hard enough for men in our culture today that none of us should go it alone. Together is better and that part of the journey begins with Christ on the other side of the cross.

Finally, I wanted to paint a picture of the transformation we go through as Christian men and provide illustrations of what it looks like to live desperately as a follower of Christ. Jesus did not promise we would be free from temptations and attacks of our fierce enemies that would attempt to lead us back into desperate places. They are always lurking in the shadows. Jesus did promise He would "never leave us or forsake us" and sent the Holy Spirit to seal our salvation and strengthen our hands for battle.

Let me close with these words of encouragement for you. ***Your life matters to God***—no matter where you are right now in your life, good season or desperate one.

If you are in a good season, let Him catch you praising Him often. Be thankful and use those blessings and favor to bless others and show them favor. They are not yours to keep, but to pass along to another desperate person. Be that "cup of cool water" for the thirsty soul to which Jesus referred.

If you are in a desperate place right now, do not give up or think our good Father has abandoned or forsaken you there. He has not because He cannot. That would make Him a liar, for on many occasions He said to His men, *"I will never leave you or forsake you."* Clinging to that promise when my spirit is weary and I cannot feel His presence, I take great comfort in His words, *"I have inscribed you on the palm of My hands and your walls are ever before Me"* (Isaiah 49:14-16).

My desperate friends, whether you are reading this today in a boardroom or a basement, a mansion or a mission, a cubicle or a cell, let those words from our loving Father bring the *help, healing, and hope* we desperately need to continue our journey Home.

Walter

ABOUT WALTER SPIRES

"Failure humbles. Success puffs up. Having experienced both, I know firsthand each one can lead men into desperate places in life. Men want answers. God has them!" So says author and teacher, Walter Spires.

"Walter has a passion for encouraging and equipping men," said Glenn Cranfield, CEO of the Nashville Rescue Mission, one of several organizations in which Walter has ministered to men over the last three decades.

After relocating his family to the Nashville area in 2002, Walter began to focus more time and attention on writing and teaching biblically-based lessons to equip and encourage men from all walks of life prisoners, addicts, homeless, executives, business owners, physicians, and even pastors.

That laid the foundation for what became a national email ministry to men around the country. It also served as the catalyst for the formation of Desperate Men, the "ministry." In 2014, God gave Walter a vision to expand this platform through the development of a website, additional speaking and teaching outlets, and social media formats to reach and teach millions of desperate men around the world.

Prior to turning his focus to menistry, Walter spent more than thirty years in the healthcare industry. He was blessed to be part of leadership teams for several medical device and healthcare delivery companies. He also used his entrepreneurial skills to launch several healthcare startup ventures.

Walter's first book, Power Tools – Build People Who Succeed in Life, was launched during a season in which he wrote and delivered programs on motivation, leadership, and building high performance people/organizations. Audiences included corporate, association, sales, and management meetings as well as ministry and church conferences and events.

Walter and his wife, Gigi, have been married 33 years and have three grown children, two of whom are married. They reside in the Franklin, TN area.

To engage Walter to speak or teach at an event, meeting, or conference, please visit our website: www.desperatemen.org or contact us at info@desperatemen.org

More About Desperate Men Ministry

To learn more about this vital ministry to men from all walks of life, please visit our website at: www.desperatemen.org.

There you will find more resources for men including lessons on a number of highly relevant topics written by Walter as well as some video segments from his teaching times.

While you are there, please consider donating to support the ongoing work of this "menistry" as we work to encourage and equip desperate men from all walks of life. Walter is known for sharing the following words with many of his audiences.

"From the C-suite to the cellblock, the boardroom to the basement, and the mansion to the mission, men from all walks of life have this one thing in common:

"All men are desperate…whether they ~~know~~ *admit* it or not."

What Other Desperate Men Are Saying About Walter Spires/Desperate Men Ministry

I have been with Men of Valor Prison Ministry for eleven years. It is a blessing having Walter Spires teach the men in our Jericho project at CCA prison and our aftercare program. Walter has an awesome gift of relating and connecting with men from all walks of life bringing hope to the hopeless and light to darkness. I too have strongly benefited from Walter's teaching. He has truly helped me to become a more effective minister for the service of God's people.
Marcus D. Martin, *Men of Valor Prison Ministry*

I believe transparency is the currency of trust. Without it, I don't believe there can be trust and without trust, you don't have a relationship. Walter Spires is hitting the nail on the head with his ministry "Desperate Men." He teaches transparency in his Bible studies and models it in his own life. Men need authentic and genuine relationships that only come when men recognize that we really are all desperate as Walter suggests.
Erik Daniels, *Executive Vice President/Principal, Ronald Blue & Company*

For many years, I've known Walter as a passionate warrior for the Kingdom of God, with a heartfelt desire to equip, strengthen, and reconcile men to Jesus Christ. Across America, our society is suffering from the dramatic increases in divorce rates, crime rates, dysfunctional families, and fatherless homes. Walter's ministry—Desperate Men—is all about reversing these trends, changing the hearts and minds of men, and bringing our nation back to God.
Larry Kloess, *CEO Private Equity Investment Firm*

I cannot begin to tell you how blessed, and convicted I am each month when I read the words God has laid on Walter's heart. God has given him a remarkable gift and he is using it for Him. I forward his messages to many men across this country and someone is always ministered to. I need to be daily reminded that *"All men are desperate ... whether they ~~know~~ admit it or not."* Our world is starving for leadership, and I thank Walter for helping to equip men to be leaders.
Robbie Fischer, *Sales Executive*

In Matthew 22, Jesus teaches us that the greatest commandment is to first love God and then to love our neighbor as our self. Walter Spires embodies this in his service to the Nashville Rescue Mission. For twelve years, Walter has consistently written and taught bible lessons to the men enrolled in the Mission's Life Recovery Program. He also organizes and hosts an annual Christmas party which has become one of the highlights of the Christmas season at the Mission. Walter is passionate in his love for the Lord and has proven to be a true friend to the Nashville Rescue Mission, especially to the staff and students of the Men's Life Recovery Program.
Currey Womack, Counselor, Men's Life Recovery Program, Nashville Rescue Mission

I have known Walter for more than a decade. His Bible lessons continue to inspire me to dig deeper into the Word. The annual Christmas event Walter leads at the Nashville Rescue Mission always gives me an even greater understanding of my abundant blessings. We are delighted to have invested in the ministry of Desperate Men to help reach men all over the world!
John Hartong, Healthcare Business Owner

I met Walter Spires soon after moving to Nashville almost 4 years ago. I was immediately moved by Walter's sincere passion and desire to minister to broken men. Walter has an incredible anointing and talent for communicating biblical truth that is understandable and inspiring. His passion is motivated by a sincere belief that God takes broken men, heals and equips them to be the godly men and leaders that He desires them to be.
Glenn Cranfield, CEO, Nashville Rescue Mission

I work with many good Christian charities. Desperate Men is one of the best. I've seen firsthand the care and love that Walter has for the brothers he helps in Jesus' name.
Louis Joseph, Healthcare Executive